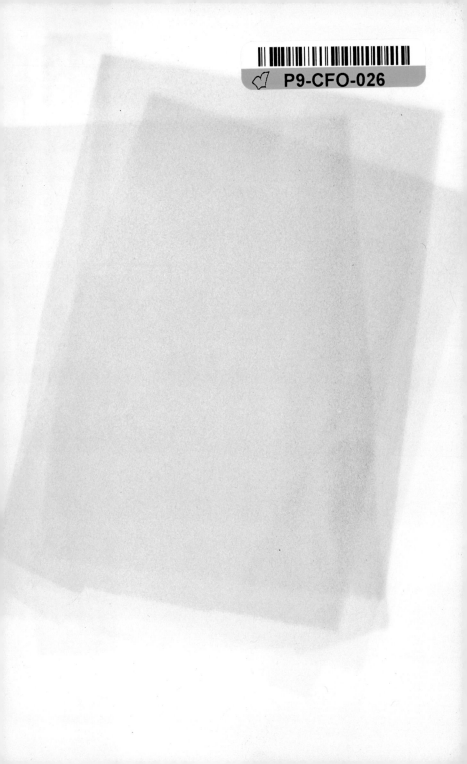

WHY I AM

A CHRISTIAN SCIENTIST

By THOMAS LINTON LEISHMAN

Our Ageless Bible

The Bible Handbook (with Arthur T. Lewis)

WHY I AM A
CHRISTIAN SCIENTIST

By

Thomas Linton Leishman

THOMAS NELSON & SONS

EDINBURGH   NEW YORK   TORONTO

TO MY WIFE

TO MY WIFE

PREFACE

T HE AUTHOR is deeply indebted to Thomas Nelson and
 Sons for the welcome opportunity which they have afforded
him both to set forth the main reasons which led him to become
a student of Christian Science and to outline some of its fundamental doctrines and practices. The performance of this task has
brought with it constant unfoldment and inspiration, and it
is hoped that these will be shared, in at least some degree, by
the reader.

In no sense does this book purport to teach Christian Science,
for in our church such official teaching is assigned to persons of
wide and rich experience, expressly trained for this important
work.

The essential source books of every Christian Scientist consist
of the Bible, together with *Science and Health with Key to the
Scriptures* and other writings of Mary Baker Eddy, the Discoverer
and Founder of Christian Science and Leader of this world-wide
movement.

This volume may be considered as a brief introduction to
Mrs. Eddy's writings and to the workings of the Church she
founded; and as a personal witness to their value and effectiveness

in the experience of an individual Christian Scientist who became
a convert to this religion after much prayerful thought, and as
the result of a settled conviction of its validity, which has grown
through the years.

The writer is most grateful to the Trustees under the Will of
Mary Baker Eddy and to the Board of Trustees of The Christian
Science Publishing Society for permission to quote from the copy-
righted works of Mrs. Eddy and from other publications of the
Society.

A brief bibliography of Mary Baker Eddy's published writings,
and of certain other books pertinent to the subject of Christian
Science, will be found on pages 239-40.

I cannot close this brief preface without a word of gratitude to
friends who have offered helpful suggestions as the book pro-
gressed, and particularly to my wife, whose support, encouragement and unfailingly constructive criticism have contributed
largely to the completion of the project.

THOMAS LINTON LEISHMAN
GREENWICH, CONNECTICUT

CONTENTS

WHY I AM

A CHRISTIAN SCIENTIST

ONE

HOW IT ALL BEGAN

I WAS NOT brought up to be a Christian Scientist, and, in fact, my whole background and training might seem to have been far removed from the way of life which I have sought earnestly to follow for many years.

That the reader may have some understanding of how and why I first became a student of this subject, perhaps I should begin by setting forth briefly the nature of my work and upbringing and how I came to follow with ever deepening interest that challenging and intensely practical study, based directly on the Bible, and outlined in the Christian Science textbook, *Science and Health with Key to the Scriptures,* by Mary Baker Eddy—in many respects the most outstanding woman of this or, for that matter, any age.

I was reared in a country manse, situated in the lowlands of Scotland, within sight of the Cheviot Hills. My father was a well-known Presbyterian minister, a scholar and writer of deep and sincere convictions. His father and grandfather were also ministers, each of whom served in his day as Moderator of the General Assembly of the Church of Scotland. I never remember a time when I did not attend Sunday School, and I have always been grateful for the basic training in the Bible and the love of it, which was constantly instilled in me by both my parents.

My mother's father was a consulting obstetrician, Professor of Midwifery and Dean of the Faculty of Medicine at Glasgow University. Her brother, Lieut.-General Sir William B. Leishman, K.C.B., K.C.M.G., F.R.S., LL.D. was Director General of the (British) Army Medical Service in the twenties. Among his many assignments he was an Honorary Physician to King George V, and is still widely remembered in medical circles for his bacteriological researches and discoveries. The London *Times* wrote of him in 1915 as one who "had placed the whole world in his debt by his splendid services upon anti-typhoid vaccination," adding that "very large numbers of men owe their lives to his efforts." (*The Times History and Encyclopaedia of the War:* Chap. XCVII) Several others among my close relatives were either doctors or ministers.

To sum up, it might well seem strange that one with such a markedly theological and medical background should choose to become a Christian Scientist, but actually—as I once wrote my parents—"I am convinced that far from deserting the 'family professions,' I am fulfilling both more fully than I could have done by becoming either a doctor or an ordained minister." As will be indicated in later chapters, the sincere student of Christian Science is joyously and inevitably committed to preaching the Gospel and healing the sick in a much broader sense than perhaps many readers would realize.

As children, religion formed a fundamental part of our lives and training, and I feel that I (as well as my sister, who later, but quite independently, became a Christian Scientist) learned even more from the example of our parents than we did from the precepts which they so conscientiously set before us.

Living within a stone's throw of Linton Kirk, one of the most historic churches in Britain, where worship had been carried on continuously for eight centuries (the original edifice was built in 1127), attendance at Church and Sunday School seemed as natural as it was inevitable, and I have never for a moment regretted the foundations which were laid within these ancient walls. There I was baptized as an infant, in a Pre-Reformation font, as was my father before me. There I took my First Communion as a newly accepted member of the Church of Scotland; there, as time went by, I preached upon occasion; and there I was married.

As school was followed by college, it is not surprising that I felt drawn to study for the ministry of the Church of Scotland, and in due course was licensed to preach by the Presbytery of which my father's parish formed a part. This period of intense theological training meant much to me, although at that time and even earlier, I was eager to understand the meaning of the various doctrines which I was called upon to accept without question. In my studies I was scholastically successful, as shown by prizes, medals, scholarships, etc., although I sensed that something vital in the way of knowledge and understanding, which I felt should be available, was eluding me. Because of this disturbing uncertainty, I consciously postponed taking what seemed the irrevocable step of Ordination, by going deeper into scholarly research. It is perhaps significant that the subject of the thesis which later earned me the postgraduate degree of S.T.M., was "The Pauline Doctrine of Justification," in which I sought to determine the real meaning of faith. Then, as now, I was convinced that Christianity was designed to be logical and practical, as well as spiritual.

After I had graduated M.A. and B.D. at Edinburgh University, the Professor of Hebrew in whose field I had been specializing, suggested that I go to Jerusalem and continue my studies there. Another suggestion was that I should take my postgraduate work at Oxford; a third, that I should pursue it in the United States— and in the end, that was what came about. It was, then, in search of further knowledge and experience that I came to New York, on a fellowship granted for one year by Union Theological Seminary, and later renewed by the Seminary for a further year.

Little did I realize, when making this decision, that like the
Pilgrim Fathers of three centuries before my time, I would find
in America a new aspect of the religious freedom which they
craved; for it was while carrying on further intensive theological
study in New York that I had my first direct contacts with Christian Science, which, through the years, has brought me a sense
of mental, spiritual and physical freedom beyond all expectation.

In Scotland I had met in passing two Christian Scientists who
were acquaintances of my parents, and I had daily walked past
a Christian Science church on my way to school in Edinburgh,
but had never attended a service, or known anything of the
teachings of this new-old religion. One of my closest friends
in New York proved to be a Christian Scientist, one who lived
what she believed and who, in the midst of all the fun and
varied activities in which our student group took part, attended
regularly the services and meetings of that denomination, not
only on Sundays, but also on week days.

The faithfulness of this student aroused my interest, and
I attended a public lecture on Christian Science, one of those
given throughout the world by authorized members of the Board
of Lectureship of The Mother Church, The First Church of
Christ, Scientist, in Boston, Massachusetts. My diary of that date
indicates that I found the lecture interesting, but I did not
pursue the subject further at that time.

Some months later, while on my way to take charge of a
summer Mission in western South Dakota, a copy of the Christian
Science textbook was loaned to me, and I was told of some outstanding instances of healing experienced by friends whom I
had grown to respect and admire. I learned that these cures,
including healings of infantile paralysis and tuberculosis and of
a broken arm and leg, had taken place as a result of conscientious
study of this amazing book and practical application of its
teachings. As I was soon to discover for myself, these teachings
are based directly on the Bible, which they confirm and explain.

My interest was at once aroused, but having majored in the

Bible and its original languages, I decided with the familiar audacity of the young student to put this new volume to the test. If it conflicted with the Bible in any way, I was determined to have none of it; but if careful study supported its claim to be based on the Scriptures and to illumine them, I would study it even more carefully with a view to making it a part of my own experience.

My first contact with this outstanding and beautifully written book proved to be the basic turning point of my life. The more I studied it, the more clear it became that so far from being a modern or newfangled treatise with scanty references to the Bible, here was a book directly and obviously based upon it—a book which took seriously the Master's explicit command that his followers in all ages should heal the sick, as well as overcome sin and preach the gospel.

My immediate and vital interest in this volume of over 700 pages is perhaps best shown by the fact that during the next few weeks—from July 1st to September 8th, as my diary shows—I read it through five times from cover to cover, gaining new inspiration and enlightenment at each reading. I preached every Sunday, but spent most of each week studying *Science and Health*.

I might add that when leaving New York a few weeks before, my plans for summer reading had been completely different. I had intended to give all my spare time to studying German and preparing for my Doctorate in Theology, which my professors had predicted I could readily have obtained within a year.

On my return to New York that autumn, I continued to study the Christian Science textbook concurrently with my theological work. Before many months had passed I had reached the unescapable conclusion that Christian Science was the faith which I must accept at all costs, and that I could not honestly remain any longer at the Seminary. This involved my voluntary resignation from the balance of a three-year scholarship which I still held from my Alma Mater, Edinburgh University. It also meant my leaving the United States, as these steps invalidated my student visa.

Thus it was that I soon found myself bound for Canada. Knowing no one there, I decided to go to the capital and took a ticket for Ottawa. In the light of my new convictions concerning Christian Science, I felt I could not conscientiously seek employment along the lines of my theological training. Consequently I was entering new territory without a job, or any direct prospect of one, but with the assurance that the stand I had taken would be justified; and so, indeed, it was, for I soon found employment in, for me, an entirely untried field, that of salesmanship. In the years since that time I have had occasion to prove the practicality of Christian Science in many different forms of endeavor, to some of which I shall refer later.

This brief chapter will, I hope, serve to explain to the reader how I made my first contacts with Christian Science; while it is my purpose in the remaining chapters, to explain something of what Christian Science is, indicating more fully why I became and why I remain a Christian Scientist.

TWO

WHAT PRAYER MEANS TO
A CHRISTIAN SCIENTIST

MARY BAKER EDDY devotes the opening chapter of her textbook to a consideration of the nature of Prayer as understood and practiced in Christian Science. The very fact that she chose to place it first among all the important topics she was about to take up shows clearly the significance she attached to it. May it not have been that she felt that while other religionists might differ in their concept of Prayer, surely all would agree on its importance, however defined. Thus "Prayer" might well be viewed as a natural point of contact in introducing to her readers the teachings of Christian Science— new in some respects, although firmly based upon what the Bible terms "the foundation of the apostles and prophets, Jesus Christ himself being the chief corner stone."

I well remember the interest and eagerness with which I first read this vital chapter, one hot July day in South Dakota, when I, as a young theological student, was on my way to act as pastor in a small prairie town for the rest of the summer. My journey involved changing trains at one of the towns in the Black Hills and a wait there of several hours. In a pine grove on the edge of town I had my first uninterrupted opportunity for quiet

19

examination of the Christian Science textbook which had been placed in my hands a day or so before.

For me, the chapter on "Prayer" provided a perfect introduction to this new field of study. As a student of theology, with a firm Presbyterian background and training behind me, I not unnaturally approached it with caution, although with an open mind, but the author's clarity of expression and breadth of outlook appealed to me from the start. There was much that had perplexed me in my theological studies and I was eagerly searching for the light, wherever it might be found. Even the Preface, so often perfunctory in other books, had already set the stage for a new adventure in religious experience by its opening assurance that "To those leaning on the sustaining infinite, to-day is big with blessings." (p. vii) Here was no call to anticipate a distant heaven—far above, or far beyond. Here was a challenge comparable to that found in the familiar words of St. Paul: "Behold, now is the accepted time; behold, now is the day of salvation." What a promise! Infinite support and sustenance from the divine source of all good awaiting acceptance this very day, together with blessings ready to unfold at a moment's notice for all willing to trust with complete confidence the eternal God!

I found the opening words of Mrs. Eddy's discussion of prayer to be equally inspiring and thought-provoking. "The prayer that reforms the sinner and heals the sick is an absolute faith that all things are possible to God,—a spiritual understanding of Him, an unselfed love." (*Science and Health:* p. 1) The wide implications of that brief sentence immediately made plain that here was a book deserving and requiring deep study, although even a cursory reading of it would provide constant food for thought.

At the very outset, then, Mrs. Eddy establishes the fact that she viewed prayer as fundamentally a complete faith not only that sin, disease and all inharmony or lack *can* be overcome by the power of God, but also that they *will* be overcome by that power. Furthermore she reminds her readers that to have its full effect such prayer must include a spiritual understanding of Deity, while its motive must be love for all mankind, love completely devoid of selfishness.

From childhood I had been taught that faith and prayer were inextricably connected and, of course, many Bible passages stress this point. Jesus himself assures his followers that "all things, whatsoever ye shall ask in prayer, believing, ye shall receive:" (Matt. 21:22) while James directly supports Mrs. Eddy's thesis, affirming that "the prayer of faith shall save the sick, and the Lord shall raise him up; and if he have committed sins, they shall be forgiven him." (5:15)

The thought of prayer including and indeed requiring a spiritual understanding of God may have been implied in my early training, but, if so, it was certainly not stressed. In fact I was brought up to believe that the various aspects of Christianity were supposed to be mysterious, and my repeatedly expressed desire for further knowledge or understanding of God, or of Christ Jesus, or of various points of Presbyterian doctrine, was silenced by a cliché which my father attributed, no doubt correctly, to Pascal: "A religion without mystery is a religion without God."

It is, of course, true that the Bible refers to "mystery" on more than one occasion, but the Greek word thus translated in the Authorized Version does not necessarily mean the inexplicable, but rather that which has not yet been fully elucidated.

Perhaps I should point out here that Christian Science is neither mysterious nor esoteric, but readily understandable because it appeals to reason and logic. It is, moreover, an essentially provable way of life adducing practical results in confirmation of its teachings, as did Christ Jesus himself, in dissolving the questionings of John the Baptist by presenting the indisputable evidence of Jesus' healing ministry. Like the apostle James, we see the value and necessity of proving our faith by our works. It has been my own experience over many years that through Christian Science the deceptive and often frightening shadows of mystery are dispelled in the light of awakened spiritual understanding—

that knowledge of the truth which, as the Master assures his followers, confers freedom.

In any event, Mary Baker Eddy's stress on the importance of thus understanding God, in the first sentence of the opening chapter of her textbook, appealed to me at once, while I later discovered that it was one of the basic points in her teaching. I had long sought to understand God and the teachings of His Son, Christ Jesus, and if Christian Science could provide such spiritual understanding, I was eager to learn more about it.

Equally provocative was Mrs. Eddy's designation of completely selfless love as a necessary prerequisite for effective prayer. So much of what passed for "prayer" had seemed to me to be largely selfish, or, at best, personal. Perhaps, I reasoned, this was why it seemed to be so seldom answered. The Christian Science concept of truly selfless prayer opened to me new vistas of thought, with the possibility of consistent results—prayer that would really work!

Significant as is the opening sentence of *Science and Health,* which impressed me so much from the start, the remainder of the chapter on Prayer and other statements by the Founder of the Christian Science movement, throw further light upon what she and her followers mean by prayer.

Christian Scientists think of prayer in terms of desire, rather than of petition, viewing it as a reverent and sincere reaching out, in the silence of their hearts, for the guidance of God in all their affairs. All too often prayer formulated in audible words has seemed to go beyond the real thoughts and purposes of the one offering it, thus lacking some of the honesty of the unspoken desire. Does not God already know the aspirations of His children before they are expressed verbally?

This in no way means that we minimize the importance, and indeed the necessity of prayer, for the eager and spontaneous communion with God which prayer implies to us is before our thought at all times. Prayer, as we see it, might be defined in part as a constant expression of uplifted thought, preparing us to accept God's ever-available bounty; or, again, it could be described as a progressively consistent attitude of receptivity, opening the way for the fulfillment of right desires.

Probably everyone has asked himself this question: What do I want or need more than anything else? What is my highest goal? What higher aim can there be than the daily practice of that type of prayer which expresses itself in the eager desire for spiritual growth, and better living, evidenced by the cultivation of love towards God and man and resulting in thoughts of kindliness and deeds of good will. When our desires are thus bearing fruit in constructive thinking and endeavor, we are surely preparing ourselves more satisfactorily for the perception and reception of God's blessings than if we merely asked for them in terms of verbal prayer, no matter how fervent and sincere our petitions might be.

As a child I was taught Paul's advice to the Thessalonians that they should "pray without ceasing," and was long troubled by my seeming inability to live up to this urgent but apparently impractical demand. Indeed it was not until I read the Christian Science textbook that I had a clear sense of what these words implied and how I could put them into practical effect. It became clear to me that to the extent that I made an honest and consistent effort not only to know God's will, but to put it into daily practice, I could obey the apostle's injunction, and learn increasingly the meaning of constant and effective prayer, not only for myself but for the world.

Perhaps one of the aspects of prayer most characteristic of Christian Science is the stress laid on recognition or realization rather than on petition, upon joyous acceptance of healing, supply, good in every form, rather than upon requests for such benefits. *Petition* or *request* would seem to suggest that the good we desire is being withheld for some reason, that we have to plead with God that He would grant whatever it is that we may seem to lack. Can our requests, however urgent, change the divine plan which God has made for His universe? Christian

Science emphasizes the fact that His giving is perpetual, completely impartial and unlimited. It is our receiving that is at fault. All good awaits our ready acceptance—our joyous realization of its presence and constant availability.

Mary Baker Eddy gives expression to this thought in a well-loved and deeply encouraging passage, the opening sentence of which appears on the walls of many Christian Science churches: "Divine Love always has met and always will meet every human need. It is not well to imagine that Jesus demonstrated the divine power to heal only for a select number or for a limited period of time, since to all mankind and in every hour, divine Love supplies all good." (*Science and Health:* p. 494) If this far-reaching statement is true—as Christian Scientists sincerely and joyously maintain—then the realization and acceptance of its implications are surely of incalculable importance.

A vivid illustration of the close connection between realization and effective prayer appears in the familiar Biblical experience of Elisha and his servant at Dothan. (II Kings 6:8-17) To his consternation, the young man awoke one morning to discover that during the night a Syrian army had completely surrounded the town in which they were lodging. Turning to Elisha for counsel in this emergency, he received the confident assurance: "Fear not: for they that be with us are more than they that be with them." Still to his servant's apprehension there was no change for the better in this hazardous situation. True, Elisha's prayer which follows is recorded in petitionary form—"LORD, I pray thee, open his eyes, that he may see"—but the result appears in terms of realization. Where the young man had formerly seen only the forces of the enemy, he now saw, closer still, the forces of divine protection, which had been there all the time—unseen by him, but already visible to the more spiritual vision of his master. "Behold, the mountain was full of horses and chariots of fire round about Elisha."

In the course of my own work and prayer as a Christian Scientist I have come to view realization as something more than the recognition of the presence of good and harmony, important as such an attitude is. The realization which I feel to be one of the bases of true and effective prayer includes the acceptance of what is real and permanent, together with the rejection of the illusory and unreal. In her exposition of Christian Science, Mary Baker Eddy says much about reality *versus* unreality. In many passages she uses the familiar and effective illustration of dreams, in which our experiences often seem to be startlingly vivid and actual; yet, in the clear light of day we become fully aware that they were purely mental, possessing little if any basis in factual experience. Such fears as we may have manifested in sleep are seen to be groundless, once we are fully awake. The dangers we encountered are proved to be unreal.

Christian Science argues that if harmony, conferred and maintained by God, infinite good, is real, then its opposite, discord, has neither authority nor power to disturb or to destroy. If health is real and God-bestowed, then sickness and disease, being diametrically opposed to health, have in the final analysis no basis in Truth or reality and consequently cannot plague man. This does not mean that Christian Scientists blandly deny the *seeming* reality of disease, nor do they look slightingly upon those who are still in bondage to this often terrifying nightmare, which appears in such varied forms. Their prayers for themselves—and for others, when their aid is requested—are designed to affirm the facts of God's presence and providence, and to maintain steadfastly the reality of good and harmony in the face of all arguments to the contrary. They realize that many do not yet see, that others are only beginning to glimpse the glorious possibilities of the Science of Christianity as applied to human problems, and that kindliness, patience and understanding are essential in introducing to the sick the age-old method of healing by prayer practiced and commended in the Scriptures, and made clear and available to all the world through Christian Science.

With a few conspicuous exceptions, such as the Lord's Prayer, which we use constantly, together with its spiritual interpretation as recorded by Mrs. Eddy, and a "Daily Prayer," which she wrote and the use of which she commended to her followers (see below, pp. 68 f. and 218 f.), our prayers are basically in thought rather than in word, a fact which, as we see it, contributes to their sincerity. Even the Lord's Prayer and our "Daily Prayer" based upon it are so thoughtfully offered that they too may be said to rise above the limitations of verbal, audible petition into the realm of an inward reaching out for God, a confident acceptance of His ever-available blessings.

Prayer, then, constitutes a fundamental aspect of the activities and aspirations of the Christian Scientist—as natural and inevitable as it is effective. In short, Christian Scientists take prayer seriously, considering it as much a necessity of their everyday activities and careers as of their inner lives. For example, an active student of this subject would not fail to turn to God in prayer before casting his vote in an election, before taking any important step in connection with his business, or before making any plan relating to his private affairs.

The basic reason for this, as I see it, lies in the fact that we do not view prayer as exclusively religious in either its practice or its effects, any more than we view Christian Science itself as just another religion or denomination. To us this Science is essentially an over-all way of living, just as the early Christians were often described as followers of "the way."

Perhaps I should explain also that in spite of our wide application of the concept of prayer to all our activities, we do not consider it as a direct method of obtaining *things,* or positions, or cures which we may want, however eagerly. To the extent that we search for and accept right ideas, that we sincerely and prayerfully desire constructive spiritual awakening and unfoldment, that we are prepared to allow God's righteous government to hold sway in our thoughts and lives, this type of prayer cannot fail to make its results manifest progressively in each varied segment of our human experience.

The greatest Teacher of all time surely provided a recipe for successful prayer when he called upon his hearers to seek first the kingdom of God, and the righteousness, or right thinking, inevitably associated with it, making it clear that in proportion to their sincerity and consistency in starting from the standpoint of this sublime goal, their various needs would be met, not in meager measure, but in full abundance: "All these things shall be added unto you." This Biblical concept of prayer, based on the desire to accept and remain under the rule of God and to attain to the thought and practice associated with His kingdom, lies constantly before the thought of the alert Christian Scientist.

While we are fully accustomed to seeing and experiencing outstanding practical results along the lines of physical healing by prayer, it is most important always to bear in mind that this represents but a relatively small portion of the widespread constructive consequences of the type of prayer stressed in the teachings of our denomination.

In answer to a question often asked of Christian Scientists, as to whether this Science is limited in its effects to the healing of disease, Mrs. Eddy herself provides an unequivocal and direct reply: "Healing physical sickness is the smallest part of Christian Science. It is only the bugle-call to thought and action, in the higher range of infinite goodness. The emphatic purpose of Christian Science is the healing of sin; and this task, sometimes, may be harder than the cure of disease; because, while mortals love to sin, they do not love to be sick." (*Rudimental Divine Science*: pp. 2-3)

It is clear, then, that the object of our prayers is not exclusively or even primarily to overcome bodily ailments, even when considered severe. This type of healing, widespread though it is among even beginners in the study of Christian Science, and welcome though it may be to an individual, is of little permanent value to himself or to society, unless he views it as a first step towards moral and spiritual progress and regeneration, now perhaps more readily available to him following the removal of the fetters of disease, and his awakening to the unlimited opportunities for good revealed by this teaching.

Many earnest students of Christian Science, having been introduced to the subject as the result of personal physical healing, have gone on to explore its higher and broader aspects which meant so much to Mrs. Eddy; but it is only fair to state that many, many others, like myself, were first attracted by its teachings—notably by its noble concept of prayer—and only later experienced its curative results as they encountered occasional physical difficulties along the way, calling for the application of this aspect of prayer.

I feel no hesitancy in affirming that no matter what the avenue through which a Christian Scientist originally approached the study of this broad and highly practical subject, he has found abundant evidences of the efficacy of prayer as understood in Christian Science. Through it a sense of injustice or resentment, grief or sorrow, weariness or anxiety, unemployment or lack, and countless other problems, can be and have been joyously overcome.

Among the widespread results of prayer, as Christian Scientists understand it, and as I have sought briefly to outline it in this chapter, one of the most important lies in the deeper understanding of God which it confers. The very habit of daily and hourly reaching out for such understanding of His will and the acceptance of His constant bounty, cannot fail to impart in increasing measure a fuller recognition of the nature of God, and the consequent recognition of the nature of man as His reflection. This has certainly been my own experience.

It has also been my experience that through the practice of prayer as inward constant acceptance, realization, affirmation and unselfish desire for unfoldment, other aspects of such prayer have developed, reaching far beyond and above my own individual desires and aspirations. Thus the type of prayer which means so much to Christian Scientists becomes increasingly associated with the universal welfare, rising beyond the needs and hopes of the individual student to the family, to the community, to the nation, to society as a whole, and to that eagerly desired goal of world peace and harmony.

THREE

GOD AND MAN AS UNDERSTOOD IN CHRISTIAN SCIENCE

OF ALL THE studies undertaken by the seeker after truth or reality, none is surely more important than the conscious and constant effort to understand God, the source of all true creation. In fact the religious status of any individual, group or nation, may well be judged by the nature of its concept and understanding of Deity.

Every group, no matter how primitive, has its God or gods, to the extent that it feels the existence of laws which it cannot control and by which it is felt to be controlled. The sense of power above or beyond the individual has often taken form in personified forces of nature—gods of storm or of water, of fertility or of drought—while to many, the sun and the moon, light and darkness, surely suggested, although faintly, governing powers.

With the gradual development of mankind through the ages have come more exalted and less naturalistic views of Deity. In the great religions of the world, the thought of many powers to be dreaded, placated or worshipped, has gradually yielded to the concept of one supreme governing power, variously named or regarded—the Brahma of the Hindu, the Allah of the Moslem, the Ahura Mazda of the Zoroastrian, the God of Jews and Christians. Yet there remain relatively wide differences in the concepts of Deity, even among students of the Bible, and my purpose in this chapter is to suggest to the reader something of what God means to the Christian Scientist—or at least to *this* Christian Scientist—and also to outline our concept of man.

The definition of God which I first learned at my mother's knee and have never forgotten, was that set forth in the Westminster Shorter Catechism: *"What is God?* God is a Spirit, infinite, eternal, and unchangeable, in his being, wisdom, power, holiness, justice, goodness, and truth"; and these familiar words did their part in forming a basis for the deeper and broader understanding of Deity which has since come to me through my study of Christian Science.

Surely any concept of the Supreme Being above and beyond that which is most crassly material, would include the thought of His being *eternal,* if the faith included followers willing to subject their belief to the test of reason. The concept of Deity as *infinite* (in its broad sense of "completely boundless and unlimited") would almost certainly find far less general support; while the third adjective, *unchangeable*—recorded in the definition set down by the Westminster divines—could scarcely be accepted in its full meaning by the countless worshippers who, in all sincerity, offer prayers of petition, imploring God for specific results, thereby expecting a change on their behalf of the divine plan.

In the writings of the Discoverer and Founder of Christian Science, however, we find again and again both definite stress on and complete acceptance of God's unchangeableness, infinitude and eternality in all the varied aspects of His being, views which bear out the highly inspired import of the Bible message as we understand it.

Those great spiritual seers, the prophets of Israel, repeatedly emphasize the value and indeed the necessity of knowing God. Thus Hosea, one of the first of the prophets to record his message in writing, was convinced that the material sacrifices so widely offered in his age could never take the place of kindliness and love,

and that "knowledge of God" was one of the primary requirements of Deity. Moreover his contemporary, Isaiah of Jerusalem,
joined with him in stressing the vital importance of knowing and
understanding God, predicting the fact that eventually their
lofty aspirations would be so widely fulfilled that the whole
earth would be "full of the knowledge of the LORD, as the waters
cover the sea." (Isa. 11:9)

It will be recalled that Moses himself, living some eight centuries before Hosea and Isaiah, was eager to learn the name of
Deity, so that he could reassure his fellow countrymen in Egypt
that it was indeed the God of their fathers who had commissioned
him to lead them out of their captivity; while throughout the
ages, theologians and philosophers alike—not to mention countless thousands of sincere individuals in every walk of life—have
set themselves a goal similar to that of the great lawgiver.

During the period of my training with a view to entering the
ministry of the Church of Scotland, and even before that time, I
myself sought earnestly for a deeper understanding of the nature
of God and for the solution of certain inconsistencies which
seemed to arise in what I had been brought up to believe concerning Him and the nature of His dealings with men.

It was but natural, then, that when I first learned of Christian
Science, I should be especially interested in finding out what it
held concerning the Supreme Being. It may be added that my
interest increased immeasurably on discovering that while, as
was to be expected, some of the names for Deity emphasized by
Mary Baker Eddy were already familiar, new and challenging
light was cast upon them, and that others, less familiar, and in
some cases almost entirely unfamiliar to me from my previous
studies, were brought to my attention. From that moment on I
made it my business to study and analyze the names for God
which Mrs. Eddy stresses, together with other significant aspects
of the divine nature on which Christian Science lays special emphasis, with a view to determining whether or not I could conscientiously accept them as justifiably outlining the nature of

God, and as providing the answer to my individual needs and aspirations.

At the risk of anticipating the conclusion which I have reached after many years of study and research, not only along the lines of Christian Science itself but also of other denominations and religions, it may be stated at this point that the definition of God presented by Mary Baker Eddy, illuminated and supported by other indications of His nature to be found in her works, has met the criteria of careful analysis which I have sought to apply to it. Moreover, the growing understanding of its various aspects has been found both inspiring and effective in the course of my daily life as a student of Christian Science.

In this connection it may interest the reader to know that the members of our faith often avoid referring to themselves directly as "Christian Scientists." Realizing increasingly the breadth and scope of this Science and its unparalleled potentialities for good, they continue to consider themselves as *students* of this vast subject, although they may have been active members of our church for many years.

To return to my original approach to the Christian Science concept of God, one of my first steps in seeking to evaluate it was to re-examine the Bible records, to which all Christians turn as a primary source for their understanding of Deity. Moreover in the light of my special interest in the original languages of the Scriptures, I naturally took them into account in my study.

One idiom found repeatedly in the Greek of the New Testament impressed me from the start, because of the confirmation it afforded of the consistent practice, found in the writings of Mary Baker Eddy, of using and capitalizing certain names for God, some of which are widely used by all Christian denominations, while others are chiefly characteristic of Christian Science.

The early uncial manuscripts of the Greek New Testament, which show little if any distinction between upper and lower case letters, were remarkably consistent in not merely naming Deity *THEOS* (GOD) but specifically *HO THEOS* (THE GOD), which

is the Greek equivalent of God—with a capital *G*. In the Authorized, Revised and Revised Standard Versions of the Bible, as in
translations prepared by individual scholars, there are repeated
instances in which *HO THEOS* is correctly translated "God."

Therefore, applying this widely accepted idiom to other passages in the New Testament, where the Greek refers literally to
"the spirit," "the soul," "the mind," etc., is there not a remarkable confirmation of and parallel to the capitalization of Spirit,
Soul, Mind, etc., as names for the Supreme Being?

I believe it will be of interest to the reader if I cite a few
specific examples of how this idiom can be applied, thereby
supporting the validity of the sublime assurance expressed by the
Discoverer of Christian Science that her teachings found support
and justification not only in the familiar English translation of
the Scriptures which we know as the Authorized Version, but also
in the languages in which our Bible was originally composed.
Further evidence to this effect will be adduced later.

In Romans 12:2, the King James translation and with slight
variations, other versions also, would indicate that St. Paul
meant, "be ye transformed by the renewing of *your* mind"; although the original Greek reads literally *"the* mind"—a phrase
which I prefer to translate "Mind," on the basis of the idiom now
under discussion. Does not this rendering cast new light on the
whole passage?

Granted that the concept of the renewing or transformation of
our minds, even on a human plane, is a lofty one, is not the
apostle's thought much more inspiring when his words are taken
in what I feel to be their original spiritual significance! Jesus had
exclaimed, "Be ye therefore perfect!" while now Paul cries, "Be
transformed by Mind's renewing"—by the uplifting, encouraging
renovating power of God, the supreme Mind or Spirit, the governing intelligence of the universe.

This constant renewing of Mind, God, may well be understood
as assuring the permanence and continuity of that state of perfection and capability which is the rightful heritage of man, the

child of God, as the Master indicates in his Sermon on the Mount. A recognition of this glorious fact inevitably transforms one's thought and experience, resulting in what Christian Scientists often call *demonstration,* that acceptance and proof of the power of God manifested in healing.

St. Paul seems to have been well aware of this, for he saw that the renewing of Mind led to transformation, followed by proof or demonstration, for he wrote, in effect, "Be transformed by Mind's renewing, that you may *prove* what the good, acceptable and perfect will of God really is."

Elsewhere the apostle writes of God as follows, according to the familiar rendering of our common version: "Now the Lord is that Spirit: and where the Spirit of the Lord is, there is liberty" (II Cor. 3:17) but, literally taken, his words are: "Now the Lord is the Spirit," or, as I see it, "the Lord is Spirit."

Similarly, when Peter calls upon the Christians of Asia Minor to "abstain from fleshly lusts, which war against the soul" (I Pet. 2:11), he may be considered as using the same idiom and thereby indicating the concept of God as "Soul."

Again, the Master's own words as recorded in John's gospel (8:31,32) could justifiably be translated as having reference directly to God as Truth. "If ye continue in my word . . . ye shall know Truth" (literally "the truth") "and Truth shall make you free."

With the exception of the term "Father" which will be mentioned later, *Spirit* possesses the distinction of being almost the only name directly and expressly applied to Deity by the Master himself. Indeed as we study the Gospels, we find that his definite statements regarding the character and nature of God are remarkably few, but bearing in mind his characteristic method of teaching, by illustration and by parable, this is not altogether surprising. May we not justly say that Christ Jesus chose to explain to his followers, in his own day and in all time to come, what God *is,* chiefly by demonstrating what God *does?*

Christ Jesus' description of God as *Spirit* which is, of course, fully accepted by Christian Scientists, suggests to me the universality of God's power and presence and it is surely significant that the Master's teaching with regard to it was given in a context showing clearly the breadth of his own thought and his freedom both from prejudice and from false nationalism.

He was talking with a Samaritan woman—a member of a national group scorned by their Jewish neighbors as half-castes, because of their partly Assyrian ancestry, while their rejection of the Old Testament, with the sole exception of the law of Moses, further separated them from orthodox Judaism. Their maintenance of a rival temple on the slopes of Mount Gerizim had, since before the time of Nehemiah, provided an additional bone of contention.

Swiftly the Master severed the chains of materialism, bigotry, hatred and prejudice by appealing to the higher law of Spirit. True religion, he pointed out, is essentially spiritual, coming from Spirit, God, and is not confined to any one group, nation or territory. "God is Spirit," Jesus declared, "and they that worship him must worship him in spirit and in truth." (John 4:24) It will be noted that while the Authorized Version reads "God is a Spirit," I am accepting the rendering "God is Spirit" upheld by most modern translators. It is true that some versions, including the Revised Standard, do not capitalize the term "spirit" but the basic meaning remains the same.

While we owe the momentous assertion that *God is Spirit* directly to Christ Jesus, the writers of the Old Testament had long before played their part in preparing for this statement. Time and again we read of the Spirit of God or the Spirit of the Lord; indeed we are told at the very outset of the narrative of spiritual creation, as given in the first chapter of Genesis, that "the Spirit of God moved upon the face of the waters."

Of special interest, however, are those many passages in which the divine Spirit is represented as guiding and governing men in *all* their affairs, whether secular or religious. Thus the book of

Exodus tells us of a certain Bezaleel, a skilled artisan who specialized in metal work and carving and whose success was directly attributed to the fact that he was "filled" with the "spirit of God." Joseph, on the other hand, was a statesman, Prime Minister of all Egypt, and we learn that he was appointed to this high office precisely because he was "a man in whom the Spirit of God is"—as Pharaoh himself put it.

One more illustration may be given, that of Gideon. The record indicates that he came from an obscure background, and operated a small farm in southern Palestine, yet "the Spirit of the LORD came upon" him. When thus inspired to wider activity, he proceeded to deliver his country from its oppressors. Then, too, prophet after prophet tells of consciously receiving the guidance and support of the divine Spirit.

Today, Christian Science, as set forth by Mary Baker Eddy, stresses with equal clarity the progress which can be manifested by individuals in all walks of life, when they, like their counterparts in the Old Testament, are willing to accept the guidance of the one Spirit, God.

It has been my own experience through many years of both business and professional life that a recognition of God as Spirit, and a conscious effort to manifest the spiritual intelligence with which God has endowed man, is of practical effect in solving problems of all kinds.

On one occasion my immediate problem was a financial one. That evening, following my usual custom, I was attending a Wednesday Evening Meeting at a Christian Science church in New York City. After paying my room rent for a week in advance, I had about five dollars in my pocket and at the same time I was unemployed. The situation seemed discouraging enough, for never before had my finances been so low. As always, the service brought me much encouragement, reminding me of how Christian Science had helped me and others to solve problems of other kinds equally pressing; moreover, I was deeply grateful for the fact that while I still had no position, and could hardly have had

less money, I did have an idea—and within a few days it began to
bear fruit.

The fact of the productivity of right ideas, when brought into
the consciousness of the individual through the recognition of
Spirit, God, as their source and inspiration, is repeatedly stressed
in Christian Science. At this time of financial lack I recalled that
on previous occasions my needs had been supplied, when I, for
my part, had done the best I could, and had been willing to
await the outcome without doubt or fear, assured that like the
writer of the twenty-third Psalm, I could not want when submit-
ting to God's guidance.

It came to me that my intensive training in the Bible and its
languages could surely be turned to good account, and so indeed
it proved. Almost immediately I was able to organize a small
group of people who wished to study the Bible with me. For
about ten years this free-lance Bible lecture work grew and prospered, and from almost the beginning I gave my full time to it.
It took me to various parts of the United States, while for several
successive summers it was also carried on in Great Britain. It
proved to be a successful and most interesting project, and I only
left it as a vocation to take up other constructive work urgently
demanding my attention.

It may interest the reader to know that over this entire period
each lecture session was carried on without a single interruption,
delay or postponement due to illness or physical disturbance, even
when carrying through the most heavy and concentrated sched-
ules. This I attribute directly to my growing understanding and
practice of Christian Science.

I mention these details to illustrate the point which Christian
Science makes, that a right idea, however small, when derived
from Spirit, God, can indeed bring supply and protection translated into the terms of our human need. Let me re-emphasize the
fact that Christian Scientists do not pray for money or jobs, but
rather for spiritual unfoldment and right ideas, for wisdom and
intelligence to take the right steps and to follow the ever-available

guidance of divine Spirit in seeking the best way to serve mankind.

The reader will surely agree that of all the aspects of the divine nature indicated in the Scriptures, the love of God is perhaps the most appealing, the most inspiring, the most comforting to those faced by the innumerable problems and perplexities which beset mankind. God's care, compassion and understanding—in brief, His constant manifestation of love—are stressed not only in the New Testament, but almost equally in the Old.

One might expect this in the writings of the great prophets of Israel, two of whom, Jeremiah and Hosea, are especially vocal in their emphasis on the love of God; or in that matchless anthology of inspired Hebrew poetry which we know as the Book of Psalms, and which constantly develops the theme of God's tender care. Yet, even in that section of the Hebrew Scriptures devoted primarily to law and history, God's love is far from being forgotten.

Deuteronomy in particular contains constant references to the love of the LORD expressed not only towards the people of Israel, but also on behalf of humanity as a whole, and its readers are urged to emulate such love not only towards their Maker, but also towards all with whom they come in contact in their daily affairs. Even Leviticus, with its primarily legalistic approach, joins with Deuteronomy in emphasizing the importance of putting into practice in human relations the love which finds its source in God, for it will be recalled that it was this book that laid down the rule of conduct which Jesus later so strongly upheld, that all must strive to love their neighbors as themselves.

It is sufficiently evident, then, that many passages in the Old Testament refer either directly, or by implication, to the love of God, assuring us of His deep and perpetually loving interest in man, His creation. But it is St. John whose understanding of this subject appears to have won for him the unique distinction of being known as the "disciple whom Jesus loved," and who not only affirms that "love is of God," but goes on to record the transcendent fact that God is not merely loving, but is Love itself.

During the course of my earlier experiences as a student at theological colleges there appeared to be little if any recognition given to the full significance of the apostle's affirmation that "God is love." Rather, as I recall, there was a tendency to consider John's thought as seeing in love little more than an attribute, however important, rather than a definition of the Supreme Being. Mary Baker Eddy, on the other hand, felt justified in accepting the apostle's statement at its face value, pointing up its implications by invariably capitalizing Love in her writings when applied to Deity, and viewing *Love* and *God* as synonymous terms.

If God Himself is indeed Love—as Christian Science so strongly maintains on the basis of the Biblical evidence—then surely there can be no limits to His expression or manifestation of that Love which might even be termed His true selfhood in action.

The consistent spirituality and sincerity of John's writings and the closeness of his association with the Master combine to suggest that in thus defining God as Love, as we understand his words, he was reflecting the teachings of Christ Jesus, while the Gospels seem to confirm this.

Jesus' whole career constituted a demonstration and consistent expression of the power and presence of his heavenly Father, divine Love. He loved little children. He loved the poor and distressed, those who were despised or mistrusted by their fellow countrymen, those who were wayward or in want. The sick and the sinful, the dying—and even the dead—felt and responded to his love.

The Master's discernment and loving appreciation are clearly illustrated in the account of the rich young ruler who came to him to know what he should do to "inherit eternal life." This young man has often been criticized for his hesitation to sell his rich estates and distribute the proceeds to the poor. He has been accused by others of boastfulness and pride in that he claimed to have obeyed the commandments faithfully from childhood. It is evident that the Nazarene was well aware of this man's limitations, but his love for him was both strong and spontaneous. The King James Version says: "Jesus beholding him loved him," which I prefer to translate "Jesus loved him at first sight!" This is one of many instances in which, through his clear understanding and reflection of the Love which is God, Christ Jesus was ever ready to see the good in those whom others despised, to love those whom others rejected.

It was typical of the Master that he loved not only his friends and neighbors, but also his most dangerous and persistent enemies and taught his followers to do likewise, while his conscious and constant expression and practice of divine Love, God, inevitably resulted in healing. In consonance with her eager desire that she and her students should conscientiously follow Jesus' example, Mrs. Eddy makes this sublime statement in *Science and Health* (p. 266): "Universal Love is the divine way in Christian Science."

Love towards both God and man formed the very foundation of Jesus' message, and he clearly regarded the practice of love in all the affairs of men, as the means by which they might best express the essential nature of their heavenly parent, divine Love, that God who, as the Master himself expressed it, "so loved the world, that he gave his only begotten Son, that whosoever believeth in him should not perish, but have everlasting life." (John 3:16)

The works of Mary Baker Eddy indicate clearly to the discerning reader that she viewed the expression of the Love which is God as one of the fundamental prerequisites for healing, in the wide sense of the restoration to, or rather recognition of man's original state of harmony. The records of her life show how time after time her loving and compassionate thought or glance, inspired by the confident assurance of the inevitable perfection of man as the spiritual image and likeness of God, were sufficient to bring relief from pain, sickness or other disability, often even to the passing stranger.

The Book of Acts implies that people were healed as the apostle Peter passed by, and Mrs. Eddy's clear reflection of the radiance of divine Love, God, brought about similar results.

Some years ago I was talking with a Christian Science practitioner who had heard Mrs. Eddy speak at "Pleasant View," her home in the vicinity of Concord, New Hampshire, around the turn of the century. Members of our denomination had gathered from all parts of the country to be present on this occasion, and my friend had the greatest difficulty in finding a room in Concord. At last she succeeded in finding lodging in the home of a Roman Catholic woman. Learning that my friend was a Christian Scientist, she related to her this personal experience.

One day she had had a very severe headache and could scarcely endure the pain. In an attempt to cool her fevered brow, she pressed it against the window pane, but obtained no relief whatever. As she stood thus, she heard a carriage coming down the street. Everyone in Concord knew Mary Baker Eddy by sight, so there could be no question as to who it was. Seeing the face at the window, Mrs. Eddy smiled at her and bowed. From that instant, the woman told my friend, the pain vanished completely, and she was free and at peace. She realized that in some way, which she could not herself understand, the Discoverer of Christian Science had brought her healing.

The recounting of this simple but significant incident, which had remained indelibly fixed in my friend's recollection, impressed me deeply at the time I heard it, so that I took careful notes of what she told me. Truly, here was one from among innumerable proofs of Mary Baker Eddy's own words in *Science and Health* (p. 13): "Love is impartial and universal in its adaptation and bestowals."

Is it not true that divine Love, and even the manifestation of that Love in human experience, to the extent of our understanding of it, can provide for all His children a protection which is secure and unassailable, when they exclude from thought the false arguments and suggestions of fear, suspicion and hatred, and think constructively in accordance with this invariable law of Love?

I had unmistakable proof of this during a visit to Palestine in 1937, when the tide of racial tension was running high and visitors like myself were warned that it was highly dangerous to visit any outlying districts unescorted. Carefully considering this well-meant advice, I recalled that—in Biblical phrase—I was clad in "the armour of righteousness," in other words, of right or constructive thinking, which I, as a Christian Scientist, sought consistently to express.

I had come to Palestine to see for myself the many sites so closely associated with the great characters of Bible times and to visualize as clearly as possible the nature of the environment in which they carried on their life work. Knowing that I had no reason to hate or fear any of the people I might encounter, whatever their race or nationality, and that they had no valid reason to mistrust me, I proceeded with my prearranged plans, not in a spirit of foolhardiness but confidently assured of the protection of Love, God.

Going alone into many outlying villages, including Emmaus and other places familiar to readers of the Scriptures, and also into the open country, I found that the friendliness and love which I sought to express were returned in kind by both Jews and Arabs, for I met with courtesy and consideration, instead of the hatred and opposition of which I had been warned, even in cases when scarcely a word could be understood on either side because of the barrier of language.

This experience provided me with practical evidence of the validity of the assurance which Christian Science gives to the effect that "the whole armour of God" which St. Paul commended is indeed freely provided by divine Love, God, for the benefit and protection of all prepared to accept it.

Love is surely the antithesis of and direct antidote for that

fear, which in all its innumerable forms, is the basis of almost all
the problems which beset mankind—including fear of disease or
lack, fear of criticism, fear of contagion, fear of the future, fear
of death itself.

The Discoverer of Christian Science fully accepted the Scriptural assurance that "there is no fear in love; but perfect love
casteth out fear" (I John 4:18). Moreover, she turned it to practical account by healing the sick and calling upon others to do
the same, on the basis of the understanding that God is Love, and
that he tenderly and perpetually supports and protects His universal family, never plaguing them with fear. She also saw that—
not coming from God, the sole creator, whose creation according
to the Scriptures was unfailingly good—all such fears are baseless,
delusive and therefore powerless.

In countless instances it has been proved that when man's
acceptance of the power of Love, God, and of the impotence of
fear, is sufficiently clear, the manifold ills attributable to fear
can and will disappear swiftly and completely.

Truth is a term or characteristic of the deepest significance in
upholding the stability and normal functioning of human society
in all its aspects; and in an infinitely deeper and more significant
sense, may we not say that it is of the very essence of Deity? His
unchangeableness, His divine justice, the constancy of His love
for all His creation, which the Scriptures repeatedly stress, surely
point to the identification of Truth, in its highest sense, as yet
another name for God—and it is accepted as such in the writings
of Mary Baker Eddy.

Not only can the Master's own words on one occasion be justifiably translated as referring to God as Truth, the source of all
integrity and freedom (see above, p. 35), but other statements by
Christ Jesus appear to support the same thought.

For example, bearing in mind the Way-shower's outspoken
denunciation of "the devil"—the very antithesis of Deity—as "a
liar" who "abode not in the truth, for there is no truth in him,"

it is surely natural to assume that he viewed God as constituting *Truth,* as surely and completely as the devil was seen as the very personification of Truth's opposite, error or evil.

The Old Testament also, as I understand it, had its part in preparing for the concept of God as Truth. As early as the Book of Numbers, we find the prophet Balaam indicating that truth is an essential characteristic of Deity (23:19); while in an ancient song, recorded in Deuteronomy and attributed to Moses himself, the LORD is described as fundamentally "a God of truth." Time and again throughout the course of his long career covering more than a century, Moses had experienced the infallible guidance of God and the fulfillment of the divine promises, and it cannot be considered as surprising if he thus glimpsed the thought of God as not only true, but as Truth itself.

God's mercy and His truth are constantly linked in the Old Testament, and it is clear that whether or not the Hebrew people as a whole specifically identified God as Truth, they unquestion-ably viewed truth as an essential aspect or atttribute of Deity.

Truth, as Christian Science employs that mighty term, is of compelling and vital significance, for this Science maintains that the Truth which is God rules out that whole tissue of mortal lies —sin, sickness, disease, death, inharmony and materiality in gen-eral—which we are accustomed to summarize under the compre-hensive name of *error.* If God is Truth, as the Bible indicates and as Christian Scientists consistently claim and affirm, then, by reflection, the continuance of man's being is assured. This in turn implies protection, support and maintenance throughout our human existence, together with the calm recognition of immor-tality.

In discussing the teaching of the "beloved disciple" in a book first published in 1901, Dr. George Barker Stevens, formerly Pro-fessor of Systematic Theology at Yale University, observes that one of the fundamental propositions of John's concept of God, was "God is life." Is there not a close similarity between this conclusion and that which Mary Baker Eddy had reached more than a quarter of a century earlier when, in the Christian Science textbook, she set forth Life and God as synonymous terms, viewing Life as one of the Biblical names for Deity?

The authority which Dr. Stevens cites for the phrase "God is life" is a verse from I John (5:20) which he translates as follows: "We know that the Son of God is come, and hath given us an understanding, that we know him that is true [God], and we are in him that is true, in his Son Jesus Christ. This one [God] is the true God, and eternal life." (*Theology of the New Testament*: pp. 569-572).

While the specific phrase "God is life" does not appear to be found in the Bible records as rendered in the familiar Authorized Version, this thought is clearly suggested in various passages. For example, the source of the life which Christ Jesus so fully and practically manifested throughout his ministry, is shown to be none other than God Himself. (John 5:26)

Similar indications appear in the Old Testament. Thus in the course of one of the closing speeches attributed to Moses, this outstanding Hebrew leader earnestly calls upon the people of Israel to "choose life," and would have them both love and obey God for this specific reason: "for he is thy life, and the length of thy days." (Deut. 30:19f.)

Surely Moses could make this assertion with profound conviction, for had he not proved for himself the practical value of knowing that Life is God! We are expressly told that when he passed away at the ripe age of 120, he still remained as strong, active and clear-sighted as ever, despite the rigors of the preceding forty trying years in the wilderness.

If *God* is Life, as the Scriptures suggest and as Christian Science insistently affirms, how can Life for an instant be lost, destroyed or even disturbed? Moreover, on the basis of this premise, would it not follow that man, as man, possesses the permanence of Life in direct proportion to the clarity of his reflection of God?

Many a time in moments of sudden danger or difficulty a persistent recognition and acceptance of the fact that God is my Life, has brought me encouragement, support, protection and freedom, and I know personally many other students of Christian Science who have had similar experiences.

The Presbyterian faith in which I was brought up laid considerable stress upon eternal life, but I gained the impression, as I grew up, that it was some kind of spiritual existence which might, perhaps, begin now, but was more likely to commence after death. In fact, the thought, as I understood it, seemed to be that the chief, if not the only way of obtaining everlasting life, was to die!

How much more reasonable and satisfactory, as I see it, is the concept of eternal Life set forth by Christian Science, which logically maintains that that which is *eternal* surely cannot start at any given point. Because of its eternality, it must always have existed, exists now, and will continue to exist, for, as Webster's Dictionary expresses it: *"Eternal,* as used of duration, strictly implies absence of either beginning or end." Thus while some forms of doctrine are inclined to limit eternal life to the future, with the possible inclusion of the present, our faith understands eternal Life as applying equally to past, present and future.

Many a student of this Science has found that when he holds firmly to the inspired realization that man, as the child of God, was never born, but has always possessed the heritage of Life, God—this has helped him to annul the limitations of heredity, showing that man as man, is not abjectly dependent upon human parentage, however noble, however humble. May one not say that dignity and dominion are his to the extent that he claims and accepts the ability to reflect God, who is Life itself, the great source of all true vitality and existence? Moreover, since man's dominion is divinely bestowed, as the Bible assures us, how can it be lost or misappropriated?

In the Old Testament the term *soul,* which occurs several hundred times, generally corresponds closely to our word *self,* or to the phrase *inner being,* and is primarily used with reference to men rather than to God. So when we read the familiar Biblical words "my soul," so characteristic of the Psalms, they are often virtually equivalent to "myself," "I" or "me." "My soul is also sore vexed," cried the Hebrew poet, "Return, O LORD, deliver my soul"—which might be freely translated, "I am in dire trouble, return O LORD, and deliver me."

Then, too, bearing in thought the close relationship between human selfhood and a material sense of things, one can readily understand why Mary Baker Eddy noted a remarkably close relation between "soul," so widely used in the Scriptures with reference to men, and "sense" which naturally arouses thoughts of sense perception, the five senses and so forth, which so generally affect the everyday affairs of mankind. On the other hand, the Christian Science textbook has much to say of Soul, capitalized, as yet another name for Deity.

It is of course true that many of the philosophers in both ancient and modern times have not hesitated to use the term soul to express the immanence and even the creativity of the power which sways the universe, without necessarily identifying that power with God; but it was Mrs. Eddy's deeply spiritual insight that enabled her to envision *Soul* as far more than a convenient philosophical concept, for she uses it clearly and consistently as a name for God.

Now while this view of God Himself as *Soul* is only rarely indicated in the Bible, there are several passages, in addition to Peter's evident reference to Soul in the Greek of his First Epistle (see above, p. 35), which tend to uphold its use by Christian Scientists as a name for Deity.

One of the most familiar of these verses is that in which God, as Soul, is represented by the prophet Isaiah as referring with joy to the work of His chosen representative, the Servant of the LORD, who is assured of His support and guidance. "Behold my servant, whom I uphold; mine elect in whom my soul delighteth."

In this, and several other Scriptural passages in which the

phrase "my soul" is directly attributed to God, is it not clearly equivalent to our word "I" in its most exalted sense, in other words, the divine selfhood or Ego, the very essence of Deity? In this connection it is surely significant that in the course of His revelation to Moses at the burning bush, God should have chosen to emphasize both His name and His nature by identifying Himself as the eternal "I AM"—another name for Deity considered of deep significance by Christian Scientists, in common with countless other students of the Scriptures.

I am convinced that most readers of this book would readily agree that an increased understanding of the nature of Deity is essential to spiritual progress. Students of Christian Science, while gratefully acknowledging growing evidences of such progress, have learned to expect, and in an increasing degree to manifest, the results of that knowledge of God commended by the prophets, in meeting the challenges of everyday life.

For example: the practical value of gaining a clearer sense of the concept of God as Soul, which Christian Science stresses, is suggested by an experience I had while lecturing in the Chicago area one winter. My schedule called for giving at least fourteen two-hour lectures a week for five weeks in succession. One Wednesday I found myself attacked by the most severe cold I could ever remember, and while I managed to attend our usual Christian Science testimony meeting in one of the local churches, it seemed quite impossible that I could lecture twice on Thursday, three times on Friday, and so on.

Recalling that although "Soul" as a name for God was widely used in Mrs. Eddy's works, it was one with which at that point in my experience I was least familiar, on returning to my hotel I became deeply engrossed in studying the references to *Soul* in *Science and Health,* with the aid of the Concordance to the Christian Science textbook. This study so lifted my thought that by morning my problem was well on the way to complete solution, and the lecture program proceeded easily, harmoniously and without interruption.

It may be of interest to record that one of the first references I had read the previous night had awakened my consciousness to the consideration of the limitless freedom conferred upon man by the perpetual activity of Soul, God, and I need hardly add that my gratitude for an increased realization of this freedom was unbounded.

As every student of the Scriptures is aware, they emphasize the fatherhood of God, and on this basis Christians of all denominations unite with members of the Jewish faith in viewing God as the Father of men. Needless to say, Mary Baker Eddy concurred wholeheartedly in this concept of Deity, considering it as indicating a remarkably tender and practical relationship between God and His children. The apostle John brought out with great clarity the implications of this relationship from the standpoint of man, with his joyous assurance to the effect that "now are we the sons of God!" In fact Christian Science maintains that such a consistent recognition of man's spiritual nature and identity as a child of God, can so transform one's thought that improvement—including healing, harmony and happiness—is demonstrable in this human experience. Moreover, this is one of the joyous manifestations of Christian Science healing.

I have long been especially interested in the fact that while the direct references to the fatherhood of God in the *Old* Testament are sufficiently clear and definite, they remain relatively few in number—appearing only about a dozen times in all—while in the *New* Testament this concept is found repeatedly and is set forth as perhaps the most distinctive name for Deity.

In the Fourth Gospel alone, God is described as Father upwards of 115 times, and some 65 times in the Synoptic Gospels, not to mention many references in other New Testament books. By way of contrast, the kingship of God, the royal aspect of His nature and activity, is constantly stressed in the Old Testament, but only rarely in the New.

In short, both Testaments speak of God as Father, both refer to Him as King. But the records indicate that perhaps the most typical concept of God in the Hebrew religion stressed the exercise of kingship; while in the religion founded by Christ Jesus, the primary emphasis is laid on the fatherhood of the Supreme Being. The majestic monarch of the people of Israel, exalted and all but unapproachable, although ruling with righteousness and equity, yields priority to the ever-loving heavenly Father of the Christians.

Do not these facts, which can only be briefly touched upon here, indicate a highly significant change of emphasis, an upward trend towards increasingly spiritual thinking?

Such a trend had already been apparent within the Old Testament itself which may well be viewed as providing a record of progressive revelation, leading on inevitably into the New Testament.

The admittedly primitive and anthropomorphic concepts of Deity such as those found in the story of the garden of Eden, related in one of the earliest sources of the Hebrew Scriptures, gradually gave way before more enlightened views of God. Extreme nationalism also yielded, slowly but surely, before the growing acceptance of Deity as God of all the earth, and Lord of the universe. Material sacrifices became less common as men learned to heed the exhortations of such seers as Hosea and Isaiah in the eighth century B.C., with their stress upon a more spiritual form of worship. The prophets who followed them played their part in setting forth more advanced views of God and man; as did the remarkable book of Deuteronomy, which is generally conceded to show clear traces of prophetic influence. Almost innumerable examples of this highly significant trend could be cited, but these may be sufficient at least to suggest its existence.

With the New Testament came still further revelation, centered in the work and teaching of Jesus himself, the greatest teacher of all time, who so fully manifested the nature of God in human experience that he could be called the Christ—the

Anointed of God. Yet his teachings were by no means unrelated to the Old Testament. Explaining and developing its highest sense of revelation, he added new and still higher thoughts from his rich store of spiritual understanding. Yet, is it not true that revelation, by its very nature, could not cease even with the Master, as John showed in his book of the same name, while other great spiritual leaders have likewise claimed the revelation granted by God Himself to those prepared to accept it in every age.

Christian Scientists are convinced that the Discoverer, Founder and Leader of their faith manifested to a remarkable degree that spiritual revelation which constantly proceeds from the one divine Source. Part of the fruits of such revelation is to be seen in certain additional names for Deity on which Mrs. Eddy lays great stress in her writings. The fact that to some extent these names may be viewed as implicit in the Biblical records, in no way invalidates our assurance that their selection and the unfoldment of their deeper significance, came to her by revelation.

The references to God as Mother or as Father-Mother, repeatedly to be found in *Science and Health* and Mrs. Eddy's other writings, may at first seem strange to many, but on further consideration may they not be said to represent a natural extension of the direct Biblical teaching concerning the fatherhood of God? For my own part, I have come to see them as providing a clear and logical explanation of the divine parenthood—God as Father and Mother at one and the same time, the complete representation of tender, selfless Love.

Now since the stress thus laid on God as Mother, or as Father-Mother is characteristic of Christian Science, let me outline briefly certain points in the Bible which may be considered as preparing for this usage.

I clearly recollect my own father, a Presbyterian minister, preaching a sermon on "The Motherhood of God," and that—if I remember correctly—long before his son became a Christian Scientist! I cannot now recall his text, but it might well have been the words of the LORD as recorded by Isaiah: "As one whom his mother comforteth, so will I comfort you," or those of the Psalmist: "When my father and my mother forsake me, then the LORD will take me up"—passages which at least hint the parenthood of the Supreme Being.

One of the clearest indications of the motherhood of God which I have found in the Hebrew of the Old Testament is in the use of the term "El Shaddai," uniformly rendered "God Almighty" in our Common Version. It is true that some scholars are convinced that "Shaddai" is derived from the root *shadad* (to express power), leading to the rendering "Almighty," but others are equally sure that "Shaddai" comes directly from the noun *shad,* meaning "a woman's breast," thus providing a further token of the tender motherhood of Deity.

Then, too, the standard Hebrew term for "God" (*Elohim*) is admittedly in the plural, which could be understood as implying two basic aspects of God's supreme parenthood—fatherhood *and* motherhood—the complete outpouring of divine Love.

It is, of course, true that we have no record that Christ Jesus ever directly used the term Mother in referring to the heavenly Parent whom he constantly addressed as Father, but this need not mean that this concept was absent from his thought, especially when we recall the tenderness and constant care which he associated with Deity, as the Gospels show.

As unquestionably the most scholarly of the New Testament writers, it is not surprising that St. Paul should point to the thought of God as Mind, not only in the expressive verse in Romans already mentioned (see p. 34), but in other passages also. While counteracting the undue intellectuality of the Corinthians, he asks, "Who hath known the mind of the Lord, that he may instruct him?", but has no hesitation in affirming, as Mrs. Eddy later did, the ever-availability of the same Mind which guided and supported the Master throughout his career, for he adds, "But we have the mind of Christ." (I Cor. 2:16)

Then, writing to the Philippians, he adds that this Mind must be claimed and accepted: "Let this mind be in you, which was also in Christ Jesus." (2:5)

What St. Paul had implied, the Discoverer of Christian Science was inspired to develop, by employing Mind throughout her writings as a direct name for God. Granted that the philosophers had from time to time written of mind as an intelligent power governing the universe, Mrs. Eddy may be said to have raised this term to a far higher significance, giving it a definitely and exclusively deific connotation, by uniformly capitalizing it, and thereby distinguishing it from so-called human or mortal mind.

It may be added that repeatedly in the pages of the Old Testament such *qualities* of Mind as wisdom, knowledge, understanding, are attributed directly to God, confirming still further Mrs. Eddy's identification of Mind with God. It was, moreover, by the exercise of such spiritually mental qualities as these that the creative Mind formed the universe, for "The LORD by wisdom hath founded the earth; by understanding hath he established the heavens." (Prov. 3:19)

To the extent that one realizes and humbly claims that divine intelligence belongs to him by reason of his creation in the "image of God," Mind, he can indeed manifest intelligence to an extent which may sometimes seem startling to those unacquainted with the teachings of Christian Science.

For example, a Christian Scientist employed by a firm manufacturing scientific instruments and radio equipment was asked to check the proofs of their latest catalogue. Her first impulse was to refuse, as it was a highly technical publication which, humanly, she could not understand, let alone correct. However, after due consideration, she accepted the assignment and proceeded to claim the availability of that intelligence which divine Mind is ever ready to impart, and which she felt sure would direct her in discovering any errors in the printer's proof.

In this spirit of confident acceptance of divine guidance, even in such an apparently mundane task as proofreading, she marked six or eight places where she rightly felt that mistakes had crept in. These were corrected by her employer and the final printing was made. She later learned that this was the first time in many years that the firm had been able to publish a catalogue containing no errors. Thus it was proved in that office that the intelligence which Mind, God, provides through reflection can and does correct error and is available at the point of need.

This illustration may further suggest to the reader the practicality of the type of spiritually constructive thinking which Christian Science upholds, on the basis of the Bible promises confirmed and stressed by the Discoverer of this new-old Science of Christianity. It is our consistent effort to follow these teachings in all our daily affairs and endeavors. The varied and constructive results obtained are in direct proportion to the breadth and scope of our thinking. This, at least, has been my own personal experience over many years.

Space does not permit of our considering further the majestic concept of God as Mind which is of central importance in Mrs. Eddy's development of her monumental discovery, Christian Science. It is sufficient to record here that it permeates all her works, and may be fully studied there with the aid of the complete concordances to her writings.

The description and acceptance of God as *Principle* by Christian Scientists has often been misunderstood, yet it may well be said to be of the very essence of Christian Science, as established by its Founder on the basis of Christ Jesus' teachings and practice, and as a direct result of the revelation which came to her receptive thought. Moreover, her presentation of this term as a description of God is surely one of her most distinctive and outstanding contributions to the understanding of the nature of Deity and of the inevitable availability of His power for the guidance and support of man.

When I first began to study Christian Science, the emphasis laid on God as Principle seemed strange to me, although I found little difficulty in understanding and accepting the use of the other names for God which this Science stresses. Bearing this in mind, it may interest the reader if I outline some of the steps which led me to see that far from being a singular or even an unwarranted name for Deity, Principle is one of deep significance and value, not cold or abstract, as one might perhaps suppose, but strong, warm and fundamental, upholding and sustaining man and the universe.

Naturally, my first question was: What justification, if any, can I find in the Bible for the use of such a name for God, when the word "principle" (at least in the singular) does not even appear once in the Authorized Version?

Realizing that this version was simply a translation, representing (as does every translation to some degree) the interpretation of the translators, I turned to the Hebrew and Greek originals, besides examining some of the ancient versions.

I soon discovered evidence which satisfied me that the concept of God as Principle was not absent from the thought of the Hebrew people. For example, I found that the Hebrew word translated "beginning" in the opening verse of Genesis, is rendered "principal thing" in Proverbs (4:7): "Wisdom is the principal thing; therefore get wisdom," and what can be more justly described as "the principal thing" than "Principle" itself!

I have given much thought to the implications of Genesis 1:1 in the creation narrative, and have concluded that the Hebrew term *reshith,* usually translated "beginning," comes remarkably close to what we call "Principle"; while the Hebrew preposition rendered "in" also means "through" or "by." Hence the original thought may well have been "Through (or 'by') Principle, God created the heaven and the earth."

There is no need to assume that Principle was here conceived of as separate from God; for if God is once admitted to be Principle, one might expect Him to execute His creative activity through, or by means of, this aspect of His own being or nature.

Two other outstanding witnesses support this thesis. The first important translation of the Hebrew Bible ever made—the Septuagint (Greek) Version—dates from about 250 B.C., at least so far as Genesis is concerned. These early scholars chose to represent the Hebrew term usually translated "beginning" by the Greek *arché,* meaning either "beginning" or "principle." (This identical Greek term appears in the plural in Hebrews 6:1, and is there translated "principles" in the Authorized Version.)

Almost as famous as the Septuagint is the Latin Vulgate, prepared by the noted scholar Jerome in the fourth century. In the opening verse of Genesis, he selected the Latin word "principium," again meaning either "beginning" or "principle."

As we have seen, the Hebrew *Elohim,* usually rendered "God," is actually a plural form, as implied in the familiar words: "And God (*Elohim*) said, Let us make man in our image . . ." (Gen. 1:26). As a Christian Scientist, I am particularly interested in an idiomatic use of the Hebrew plural which may well be viewed as supporting Mrs. Eddy's inspired identification of *Principle* as a synonym for God. This can best be explained by the use of an example. The usual Hebrew word for "living" is *chay* (in the singular), but when it appears in the plural (*chayyim*), the meaning changes to "life" itself, the vital principle, which is obviously a deeper, broader, more significant word than "living."

Scholars generally describe this as the "plural of abstraction" but I feel there is equal justification for referring to it as the "plural of principle" and for viewing it as providing further evidence in favor of using "Principle" as a name for the Supreme Being.

The deep significance which Mary Baker Eddy attached to *Principle* is clearly shown in many passages in her writings, in which she considers the acceptance of this name for God as the very foundation of a scientific understanding of the great Cause of all existence.

Why, one may ask, is the name *Principle* considered of such deep importance that we apply it exclusively to God? One reason which particularly appeals to me is the fact that the words used to express this concept in Hebrew, Greek and Latin suggest clearly that which is first in both time and authority—that which is basic, certain, changeless. When thus considered, *Principle* is surely a justifiable and highly significant name for Deity, indicating that in His capacity as Principle, He is the source and changeless foundation of His creation. Moreover, does not Principle, in its deific meaning, provide for man the stability and assurance which he so eagerly desires?

The young student of mathematics may make mistakes in figuring the problems he is asked to solve, but these errors never affect the fundamental rules of mathematics. Two plus two always equals *four,* no matter how many students put down *five* as the sum. The same is true of more complicated mathematical operations. In that field they represent an established basis or series of bases, remaining effective in all circumstances, languages or countries. Similarly to name God as Principle, in the broadest and highest sense, is surely to regard Him as the eternal, invariable basis of perfection—the source and support of His spiritual creation. So universally applicable is the concept of God as Principle that it can become intelligible under any and all circumstances, and to those of any or no religion.

The supposition sometimes held that Principle gives an impression of coldness or hardness is readily offset by the assurance which Christian Science gives that Principle, as a name for Deity, is none other than Love itself.

Although this connection between *Principle* and *Love* was not clear to me at first, I came to see that surely one of the connecting links was *Law.* All true law is based upon Principle, and may it not be that St. Paul was virtually connecting Principle and Love when he affirmed (Rom. 13:10) that "love is the fulfilling of the law?" Paul, like John and other Biblical writers, followed Christ Jesus in viewing love as basic in Christianity, and as necessarily including both steadfastness and stability, which are also inherent in the term Principle. Therefore Love and Principle in their higher sense, considered as defining Deity, surely need not be viewed as in any respect antagonistic, but rather as complementary, for does not Love include the stability of Principle, while at the same time, Principle, in its deific meaning, may well be said to include the tenderness of Love?

The objection sometimes brought forward to the effect that Principle as a name for God, is altogether too impersonal, is valid, as I see it, only from the standpoint of human personality, which by its very nature is incapable of fathoming the heights or depths of Deity. How could the infinite and immortal God be adjudged personal in any limited, mortal use of the term? It will surely be admitted that divine Principle, God, could never be swayed by the whims and follies, likes and dislikes, attendant upon human personality, but rules righteously, impartially, and lovingly over all.

Many of the problems which we all encounter from time to time in human relations seem to be based upon a sense either of personal good or personal evil, often involving individuals described as "unprincipled" or "with no principles." I myself have found repeatedly that a realization and acceptance of the impersonal yet ever-loving operation of divine Principle aids immeasurably in overcoming such problems.

It is but natural that God as Principle should be viewed as establishing and enforcing His righteous demands, providing a constant standard of perfection, a goal towards which to strive, by setting forth the divine law for the guidance, support and protection of man.

It is, I am sure, scarcely necessary to point out to the reader that in the space at my disposal it has been impossible for me even to touch upon countless aspects of the nature and power of God, as revealed to the inspired thought of Mary Baker Eddy. Granted that to attain to a full knowledge of God is admittedly an infinite task, I know of no better way of approaching it than by the direct study of the Bible and of *Science and Health with Key to the Scriptures,* the two textbooks of the Christian Scientist.

Let me close this portion of the present chapter by quoting one of the concise and deeply illuminating definitions of God formulated by Mrs. Eddy. It appears on page 587 of *Science and Health,* in the chapter entitled "Glossary," and reads as follows:— "GOD. The great I AM; the all-knowing, all-seeing, all-acting, all-wise, all-loving, and eternal; Principle; Mind; Soul; Spirit; Life; Truth; Love; all substance; intelligence."

Closely associated with the Christian Scientist's concept of God, is his understanding of man, as His child, the object of His tender care.

From my early Sunday School days I was puzzled by the two accounts of creation in Genesis and questioned the reason for the striking differences and even contradictions between them— to the consternation of my teachers, who assured me that such points should not be raised.

In college I soon learned the now generally accepted explanation that the variant accounts came from different periods and represented different concepts. Genesis, chapter one, presents God as the Creator, affirming that all was good in accord with His divine planning. Developing this exalted thought, the writer or writers view Deity as creating man in His own image and likeness, to reflect or express Himself. The original being infallibly good, the image or reflection would of necessity be good also.

On the other hand, early in what is now the second chapter of Genesis, we find an entirely different picture of man, as made by the LORD God from dust or clay. As might be expected from such a beginning, difficulties and inadequacies soon arose indicating that, from the standpoint of this writer, man was primarily material, even though "the breath of life" was "breathed into his nostrils."

Genesis, then, offers two contrasting views of man: man, on the one hand created directly by God to express Himself, to reflect His perfection; man, on the other, founded on a frankly material basis, and with all the dire potentialities of evil. True, each of us appears to be faced with the choice between these two conflicting presentations of manhood; but the inevitable questions arise: Which is fundamental? Which presents the true picture of man, of which the other is the counterfeit? Is man faced with the problem of a purely material origin which he may be able progressively to overcome? or, is he basically spiritual, with the task and reward of realizing and maintaining his inherent spirituality—his true likeness to his Maker?

Christian Science, accepting as basic the account of man's creation given in the first chapter of Genesis, affirms and maintains man's permanent spiritual relationship to his creator, and sees in the contrasting record of the second chapter, not the fact, but the falsity of creation.

This does not mean that we ignore evil, or the material tendencies and heinousness of sin which would seek to engulf mankind. Far from it! Rather do we, through ascribing all power to God, good, deny evil the right to claim any power. In taking a firm stand against all evil and its specious claims to authority, we accept wholeheartedly the implications of Genesis 1:26,27 which indicate that man is always, in reality and in fact, God's image and likeness—assured that in the progressive acceptance of this deeply encouraging Biblical assertion lies the basis of man's harmony, if you will, the secret of his salvation. "And God said, Let us make man in our image, after our likeness. . . . So God created man in his own image, in the image of God created he him; male and female created he them."

It may be of interest to note that although I had read these words from childhood, I believe that what first opened my thought to their perennial significance was a statement made by Professor William P. Paterson, D.D., Dean of the Faculty of Divinity at Edinburgh University and a staunch Presbyterian. One day while lecturing to his class, of which I was a member, he reminded us that "actually, here and now, man is made in the image and likeness of God." This affirmation so impressed me at the time that I recorded it verbatim, but it was not until a year or two later, when I became a student of Christian Science, that I began to glimpse its practical effectiveness.

We feel that as Christian Scientists it is our task and our privilege to claim our inheritance, to prove for ourselves that we are indeed individual expressions of our Maker, and that harmony in all its forms is the natural heritage of man. It goes without saying that we in no way claim that this heritage is limited to our denomination, but we rejoice to explain and to share with all who will listen, what we feel to be the way to lift mankind out of materiality and lack by claiming what already exists—spirituality and abundance, health and harmony, God-bestowed and therefore God-maintained, in spite of any evidence to the contrary.

When preparing the textbook of Christian Science, Mary Baker Eddy was, of course, fully aware of the contrasting theories concerning the nature of man, and saw the necessity of stating clearly her position on this important and controversial subject. For example, she dared to challenge the importance and indeed the very existence of the material elements popularly regarded as constituting the necessary component parts of the "children of men," such as brain and muscle, heart, blood and the like.

It will surely be admitted that if one accepts fully (as Christian Scientists do) the premise that man was created in the image of God Himself, combined with Christ Jesus' assurance that God is Spirit, he must thus conclude that man is spiritual, not material, and further that he is not a frail mortal, constantly and all but inevitably, yielding to temptation. The practicality of this conclusion is indicated by the fact that its acceptance has led directly and repeatedly to the manifestation of healing and harmony, in place of sickness and discord.

This has been my own experience and that of countless other sincere students of Christian Science, and has so uplifted thought concerning even what is commonly described as the human body, that the tendency towards disease or accident is virtually eliminated. In short, we waken from the dream of materiality which results in such erroneous conditions. A recognition of man's real entity and being as the idea or reflection of Mind, God, elevates our thoughts concerning ourselves at this present stage of experience, with practical and constructive results.

Long centuries ago the Stoics maintained that "not things, but our thought of things matters"; while the familiar words of Shakespeare readily come to mind: "There is nothing either good or bad, but thinking makes it so." These, and many similar statements which could be cited do not, of course, approximate to Christian Science as taught by Mary Baker Eddy, but they do serve to indicate the widely accepted fact that the thought or concept of anything, or of any situation, is of vital importance. When our concept of ourselves and of our true spiritual nature and existence as indicated in the Bible, and stressed by Christian Science, is clearly and consistently held, we have opened the door to true progress and development.

Christ Jesus' natural and inevitable sense of his oneness with God was so clear, his recognition of his own expression of Deity so consistent, that he seems to have seen and felt the deepest potentialities of those around him, claiming and asserting that they too were God's children. In the light of his understanding of the true nature of man as a child of God, the dark shadows of sin, sickness and even death itself vanished, and healing in the broadest sense resulted. His piercing spiritual vision penetrated the various disguises which sought to cloak the spiritual selfhood of those whom he encountered. He saw them as they really were and always had been, as made in the image of their heavenly Father-Mother—not as lepers shunned by society, cripples ignored by the passing crowd, or harlots scorned by rich and poor alike. He brought them hope and healing in exchange for faith and repentance.

In one brief paragraph, Mary Baker Eddy presents a matchless summary of the Master's method of teaching and healing, which at the same time points up her own concept of what man is in reality. It is this enlightened concept of man which Christian Scientists seek to obtain and to retain at all times, and which they gladly recommend to those who would share in the enjoyment of the constructive results which inevitably flow from it.

Mrs. Eddy's words, which appear in *Science and Health* (pp. 476-77), are as follows:

"When speaking of God's children, not the children of men, Jesus said, 'The kingdom of God is within you;' that is, Truth and Love reign in the real man, showing that man in God's image is unfallen and eternal. Jesus beheld in Science the perfect man, who appeared to him where sinning mortal man appears to mortals. In this perfect man the Saviour saw God's own likeness, and this correct view of man healed the sick. Thus Jesus taught that the kingdom of God is intact, universal, and that man is pure and holy. Man is not a material habitation for Soul; he is himself spiritual. Soul, being Spirit, is seen in nothing imperfect nor material."

FOUR

CHRISTIAN SCIENCE CHURCH SERVICES

WHEN I first wrote my mother—who, the reader may recall, was the daughter of a doctor and the wife of a Presbyterian minister—that I had become a student of Christian Science, one of her immediate questions was: "What can you tell me about your services?" This chapter may be described as an expansion of my reply.

Simplicity is one of the most outstanding characteristics of Christian Science services and meetings, a fact which focusses attention upon the content, rather than upon the externals of our worship. This simplicity, we feel, has a beauty of its own, which contributes to the quiet harmony of these services.

The same Order of Service, established by Mary Baker Eddy and found in her *Manual of The Mother Church,* is followed in all Christian Science churches throughout the world, making for unity of thought and practice, and enabling the student to feel instantly at home wherever he may be.

It may be well to begin by clarifying the terms First and Second Reader, as they will be mentioned frequently when describing our services, in which they take an active part. They are officers of the church, elected usually for a period of three years, from and by the membership in the case of branch Churches of Christ, Scientist, and by The Christian Science Board of Directors, in the case of The Mother Church, The First Church of Christ, Scientist, in Boston, Massachusetts.

Following a prelude of appropriate organ or piano music, the Sunday morning service opens with a hymn selected from the *Christian Science Hymnal,* and sung by the congregation. (When a second service is held, it is a repetition of the morning service.) One of the points first noticed by the visitor is that our churches do not have choirs, a fact contributing to the heartiness and unanimity of the congregational singing—a characteristic part of our worship. We thus express our joy and gratitude, our praise and thanksgiving to God for His goodness directly and personally, rather than by proxy. Despite the beauty of the music provided by a choir of trained voices, I have observed that it sometimes tends to overawe the average churchgoer, to the extent that either he does not sing at all, or, if he does so, he doubts his ability to reach the desired musical standard.

In the *Christian Science Hymnal,* used in all Christian Science services, a great many hymns well-loved by Christians of all denominations may be found, while it also includes seven hymns written by Mary Baker Eddy, and others written by other Christian Scientists.

Much care was taken during the preparation of the current revision, which appeared in 1932, to assure the high musical caliber of its tunes and their suitability for congregational singing. The committee appointed by The Christian Science Board of Directors to prepare this new edition bore in mind that it was designed to be used in Christian Science churches throughout the world, and not merely in the United States, where Christian Science was first established. Thus it contains a number of fine tunes originating in England, Scotland, Wales, Scandinavia, France, Germany and other countries (fifteen in all), including some beautiful Hebrew melodies and tunes already internationally familiar. In some cases, the wording of well-known hymns has been slightly changed (with, of course, proper permission) to correspond more closely to the teachings of Christian Science.

Our Hymnal as a whole reflects the care given to the selection of both words and music and expresses harmony in a broader sense than that usually limited to music itself. Many a Christian Scientist, including the writer, can bear witness to the uplifting and healing message of these hymns, whether sung aloud or read as poetry.

There is such deep meaning in the wording of the hymns written by Mary Baker Eddy that it is customary in Christian Science churches to include one of these at each Sunday service, and it is read in its entirety by the First Reader before being sung by the congregation.

Following the opening hymn, our Sunday services continue with a Scriptural Selection from the Authorized (King James) Version of the Bible, chosen and read by the First Reader, who conducts the services. This reading is designed to follow the theme—but not to provide the text—of our *Lesson-Sermon,* which will be described shortly.

Presumably every churchgoer, no matter what his denomination, is accustomed to hearing hymns, prayer and readings from the Bible, but many may be less familiar with a brief period of *silent prayer* which comes at this point in the Christian Science service.

Following this brief but impressive period of reverent silence, the congregation—led by the Second Reader, who shares the platform with the First Reader—repeats audibly that concise masterpiece of prayer which holds its unique place in Christian worship as having come from the lips of the Master Christian—the Lord's Prayer; while after each clause, the First Reader alone repeats its spiritual interpretation, as given at the close of the chapter on *Prayer* in the Christian Science textbook.

The very familiarity of the Lord's Prayer, which every Christian knows by heart, sometimes has the unfortunate effect of lessening its significance. In Christian Science churches this great prayer (Matt. 6:9-13) is always repeated slowly and thoughtfully.

So far from detracting in any degree from the well-loved phrases of the Bible, the dignified and reverent comments upon them set down by Mary Baker Eddy enhance their beauty and significance, when understood, by revealing hidden depths in the Lord's Prayer, and pointing up some of its vast implications.

Mrs. Eddy writes (*Science and Health:* pp. 16, 17): "Only as we rise above all material sensuousness and sin, can we reach the heaven-born aspiration and spiritual consciousness, which is indicated in the Lord's Prayer and which instantaneously heals the sick.

"Here let me give" (Mrs. Eddy continues) "what I understand to be the spiritual sense of the Lord's Prayer:

Our Father which art in heaven,
> *Our Father-Mother God, all-harmonious,*

Hallowed be Thy name.
> *Adorable One.*

Thy kingdom come.
> *Thy kingdom is come; Thou art ever-present.*

Thy will be done in earth, as it is in heaven.
> *Enable us to know,—as in heaven, so on earth,—God*
> *is omnipotent, supreme.*

Give us this day our daily bread;
> *Give us grace for to-day; feed the famished affections;*

And forgive us our debts, as we forgive our debtors.
> *And Love is reflected in love;*

And lead us not into temptation, but deliver us from evil;
> *And God leadeth us not into temptation, but de-*
> *livereth us from sin, disease, and death.*

For Thine is the kingdom, and the power, and the glory, forever.

*For God is infinite, all-power, all Life, Truth, Love,
over all, and All."*

It is on this transcendent note of the allness of God, that Christian Scientists reverently and gratefully bring to a close the portion of their Sunday services devoted to prayer, assured that such a recognition of the nature and perpetual activity of Deity cannot fail to find its answer in inspiration and healing.

Following the repetition of the Lord's Prayer, and of its spiritual interpretation, the congregation joins in singing a hymn, often one of those written by Mary Baker Eddy, which is followed by the reading of announcements regarding Christian Science services, lectures, or any related activities of our church.

Next in order comes the solo, which takes the place of the anthem sung in many churches of other denominations. In selecting a soloist, one of the prime requirements of our church is that, in addition to good musicianship, the words to be sung must be not only inspirational, but well enunciated, so as to be clearly understood. One of the aims of Christian Science services throughout their various parts, is to bring out clarity, so that all who attend may have an opportunity of hearing and understanding the message conveyed.

The central portion of the Christian Science Sunday service is what we call the *Lesson-Sermon,* which follows the solo, and is read by the two Readers—generally a man and woman. The Second Reader reads from the Bible, while the First Reader reads correlative passages from *Science and Health.*

In the early days of Christian Science, there were personal pastors or preachers, but as time went by it became increasingly clear to the Founder of the movement that for all their sincerity, there was sometimes a tendency for an undue sense of personality to develop which would detract from the fundamental teachings of Christian Science, as found in the words of the Bible and of *Science and Health.* Therefore, in 1895 she ordained these two books as pastor of all Christian Science churches, and it became the rule in The Mother Church, and the custom in all branch churches of our denomination, for each Reader to hold office for not more than three years.

This rule has proved to be both wise and practical. It carries out the essentially democratic purpose of our church organization, enabling many of our members to share for a period in the truly rewarding work of readership, afterwards returning to continue their service as active members of the congregation.

The references used in the Lesson-Sermon are printed in the *Christian Science Quarterly,* one of the publications of The Christian Science Publishing Society, and are selected by a Bible-Lesson Committee which meets in Boston, the headquarters of the Christian Science movement. From this central point, either directly or through Christian Science Reading Rooms, these Quarterlies are distributed well in advance to churches, and individual students of Christian Science throughout the world. Consequently the same Lesson-Sermon is read on any given Sunday in all Christian Science churches in all parts of the globe.

The subjects of the Christian Science Lesson-Sermons are twenty-six in number and are thus covered twice each year. To one unacquainted with them, this might perhaps suggest a somewhat limited field of subject matter; but experience in studying them regularly over many years, has proved to me that this is far from being the case. The subjects were originally selected by Mary Baker Eddy herself, who unquestionably bore in mind the scope which each one would provide. The mention of even a few of the titles of these Lesson-Sermons, listed in full in each issue of the *Christian Science Quarterly,* will readily indicate to the reader the unlimited possibilities for development under such headings: "God," "Sacrament," "Love," "Christ Jesus," "God the Only Cause and Creator," "Doctrine of Atonement," "Christian Science."

Those well acquainted with the Scriptures already know the wealth of inspiration and the many and varied incidents and teachings which they contain, while similar riches are found in abundance within the pages of the Christian Science textbook, and as already noted, it is from these two books exclusively that the references in our Lesson-Sermons are drawn. Week after week they open to the student new and challenging avenues of thought, new aspects of the true nature of God and of man.

One of the characteristics of these Lesson-Sermons is that, as their very name implies, they are not merely *sermons*—they are also *lessons*, designed to be studied daily by Christian Scientists through the week preceding the Sunday on which they are read in church. Thus the reading at the Sunday services represents the culmination of a week of consistent study not only by the Readers, but also on the part of a majority of the congregation. So far from making the Lesson-Sermon unduly familiar, this advance preparation opens the way for new and sometimes unexpected unfoldment of ideas at the Sunday service. Not a small part of this further unfoldment is due to those other elements which, added to the Lesson-Sermon, go to make up the whole service, such as the Scriptural selection, hymns and solo.

Remembering the consistent use of the Sunday lesson by Christian Scientists throughout the world, all studying the same subject at one time, I like to recall that when the early Christians were "with one accord," they experienced the descent of the Spirit of God, and felt its results in inspiration, activity and progress, which are indeed among the fruits of our daily Lesson-Sermon.

I am not aware of any other denomination which has laid out for its members such a consistent course of study, continuing year in year out without intermission. This study is by no means limited to the reading of the Christian Science textbook, for at least equal emphasis is laid upon the Bible itself, the foundation of all Christian teaching—the basic and primary textbook not only of Mrs. Eddy herself, but also of all who accept her interpretation of Christianity.

This consistent weekly study is, then, one of the most characteristic aspects of Christian Science and one of the prime reasons

for its steady and successful development. Many other churches
can bear witness to the spiritual impetus which they have felt
among their members as a result of studies during Lent or
Advent or at other special seasons of the church year. We rejoice
in such evidences of spiritual progress, wherever and whenever
found, while, for our own part, we strive to make each day a
special season devoted to consecrated study, with our Lesson-
Sermon as its focal point, thereby raising the standard of our
individual thinking and activity and contributing to the over-all
progress of our community, our country and our world.

In most churches the sermons preached have been prepared
for delivery to a given congregation. To some extent this is true
even when the sermon is to be broadcast, since it is presumably
designed to meet the need or arouse the thinking of those within
a given district or country.

The fact that the selections used in the Christian Science
Lesson-Sermons are always prepared for world-wide use, sets them
in a class by themselves. They deal with subjects of universal
significance and, being presented without comment, offer to the
individual the stimulus of interpreting them for himself and
making their inherent message applicable to his own experience.

The very impersonality of their presentation is one of their
most valuable assets. Each lesson provides a challenge and an
opportunity for us to grow and advance as individual Christians
and Christian Scientists—and as members of a world community.

Although planned many months in advance, these lessons
are remarkably timely and are found to be applicable to current
situations and problems which could not possibly have been
foreseen at the time when the selections were originally made.
One reason for this might appear to be the breadth with which
each Lesson-Sermon is handled, but above and beyond this, the
real reason is surely to be found in the undeniable evidence of
the Word of God, present not only in the Bible, but also in this
remarkable textbook of Christian Science.

If "Jesus Christ" is indeed "the same yesterday, and today,

and for ever" (Heb. 13:8), it is inevitable that the Bible teachings which he either inaugurated or upheld, and which Christian Science sets forth for practical use in the solution of the daily problems of mankind, should likewise be viewed as timeless and universal in their application. Christian Science, as its adherents understand and practice it, is as truly ancient as it is modern— as every aspect of basic truth must be. It was indeed a discovery, not an invention, and includes, in addition to the direct revelation which came to its Discoverer, a restatement and practical explanation of age-old truths already established.

The fact that *Science and Health* was founded on the Bible teachings by its author, makes the coordinated use of these two great books in the Lesson-Sermon not only possible, but completely natural. The development of the subject therefore, can, and does form a unified whole, bringing clarification of Bible passages which may sometimes have appeared obscure, and throwing light upon the practical application of the healing and saving message of the Scriptures, helping the student to see how the Bible promises are still living and applicable today, as surely and effectively as in the Biblical era.

The main body of every weekly Lesson-Sermon consists of six sections, each of which takes up some separate aspect of the current subject, developing and explaining the theme of the lesson.

Naturally, attention is focussed upon the topic in hand, but logically related subjects are often considered, opening new horizons of thought and indicating some of the countless ways in which the main subject itself can be studied and applied.

Lest the inquirer should imagine that the use of six sections implies that one is supposed to be studied on each of the six weekdays, and the complete lesson only on Sunday, it may be explained that this is by no means the case. It is intended that the lesson be studied each day in its entirety, in preparation for the Sunday service.

Before beginning the Lesson-Sermon itself, the First Reader

reads a brief introductory note, which appears in the *Christian Science Quarterly*, explaining that the only preachers of our denomination are The Bible and the Christian Science textbook, and pointing out that the carefully selected readings from these two deeply spiritual books do indeed provide a sermon in a peculiarly real sense—a sermon free from personal interpretation and designed to be of the widest possible interest and application in meeting the needs of our age, and, for that matter, of any age. Consistent study of these lessons over a period of many years, has renewedly convinced me of the justification of such claims.

The structure or organization of each Lesson-Sermon is found to have an interest of its own. Naturally the subject for the day is announced first and is followed by the reading of the Golden Text by the First Reader alone. This brief passage from the Scriptures, rarely more than a single verse, sets the keynote for the Lesson-Sermon, indicating at the outset its Biblical basis. Next comes a Responsive Reading, also selected from the Scriptures and read alternately by the First Reader alone and by the Second Reader joined by the congregation.

Following the announcement by the First Reader at the close of the Responsive Reading, to the effect that the citations now to be read constitute our sermon, the Second Reader reads from the King James Version of the Scriptures the passages selected for the Biblical part of the first section of the Lesson, announcing that they are from the Bible, and prefacing each with the name of the Bible book from which it comes. The First Reader then introduces his (or her) reading with the clear announcement that the passages now to be read are from the Christian Science textbook, *Science and Health with Key to the Scriptures* by Mary Baker Eddy. Thus it is made perfectly clear to all, at the beginning of the main portion of the Lesson-Sermon, that one group of readings is from the Scriptures and the other from the textbook of Christian Science.

Thereafter the Readers continue to read alternately the passages chosen to form the second and following sections.

My own experience of acting as First Reader in a Christian Science branch church has been that when, after long and careful study of each Lesson-Sermon during the preceding week, I have my part in reading it aloud at the Sunday service, I invariably gain new inspiration from the reading. In fact, progressive unfoldment is one of the most constructive results of thoughtful study of the Christian Science Lesson-Sermons. By *unfoldment* I mean the development of constructive ideas and ideals, leading to progress not only in spiritual thinking, but also in the direct solution of the varied problems arising in our human experience.

The reading of the Lesson-Sermon is followed by an appropriate organ or piano selection which serves as an Offertory, and by a further hymn from the Christian Science Hymnal.

Before pronouncing a suitably selected Benediction, and while the congregation remains standing, the First Reader reads a deeply significant passage from page 468 of *Science and Health* which Mary Baker Eddy has entitled *the scientific statement of being,* together with three closely correlative verses from the Bible to be found in I John 3:1-3.

The scientific statement of being presents a concise and fundamental summary of the teachings of Christian Science concerning God, man and the universe, and will be cited in full in a later chapter (see pp. 110 f.). It is sufficient to say here that it affirms and maintains the allness of Spirit, God, and the nothingness of matter, reaching the logical conclusion, based on these premises, that God's creation, man, is always and only spiritual, not material. Equally significant, equally basic, is the assurance of the apostle John that man's sonship, as a child of God, is a present reality, not merely a future possibility.

It is indeed fitting that our Sunday services should always close on this high note of hope and faith, emphasizing the fact that man as man partakes of the unfailingly spiritual nature of his heavenly Father, divine Spirit—and reaffirming the triumphant pronouncement of St. John that our God-bestowed sonship is in effect now and for ever, a fact which automatically results, as the apostle goes on to point out, in self-purification.

Twice a year, when the subject of the Lesson-Sermon is "Sacrament," the order of service in all Christian Science branch churches varies somewhat from that which is used on other Sundays through the year and which has just been outlined.

While Christian Scientists do not have Communion Services in the sense generally accepted by many denominations, as involving the literal sharing of bread and wine in memory of Christ Jesus' last supper with his disciples, they do meet in branch churches of their denomination twice each year to turn their thoughts more especially towards union and communion with their heavenly Father.

One main difference between the order of service in Christian Science branch churches on the semi-annual Sacrament Sundays, and that used at our other Sunday services, is that after the reading of the Lesson-Sermon, the First Reader invites the congregation to kneel in silent communion with the one God of the universe, followed by the repetition of the Lord's Prayer in unison. The simplicity of this reverent act of communion is equalled, to our understanding, only by its deep spiritual significance, indicating our recognition of the unity which inevitably exists between God and man, made in His image, as the Bible teaches.

Another significant variation from the usual order of Sunday services in our branch churches, is the reading by the First Reader on "Sacrament Sunday" of the six Tenets of The Mother Church, which, although not constituting a Creed, in any formal sense, do set forth a brief outline of the main points of the religious teaching of Christian Science. (See page 104.)

In addition to its Sunday service or services, The Mother Church and each of its far-flung branches holds a Wednesday meeting, usually in the evening, although, in some instances, particularly in the case of large city churches, an additional meeting is held at noon, and is widely attended by business people and visitors.

In various respects, the Wednesday meeting is less formal than our regular Sunday services, but it has its own unique significance and value. It is at this weekly meeting that Christian Scientists and visitors—who are always most welcome—have an opportunity of hearing, and giving, personal accounts of the way in which Christian Science has aided in solving questionings and problems of those who speak, and above all has brought them a deeper understanding of God.

After an opening hymn from our Hymnal, the First Reader reads a series of passages selected from the Bible, followed by correlative passages from *Science and Health*. These readings differ from the Lesson-Sermons read at our Sunday services, in various ways. For one thing, the Lesson-Sermons, as already explained, are prepared in Boston by a specially appointed committee and take up in rotation a series of subjects selected by Mary Baker Eddy because of their over-all importance and the innumerable ways in which these broad subjects—such as "God," "Man," "Spirit," etc.—can be developed.

The choice of topics to be covered in the Wednesday readings, however, is left entirely to the discretion and inspiration of the individual First Reader, and therefore they are prepared for one church only, that which the Reader has been elected to serve.

Again, the Lesson-Sermon, being a *Lesson* as well as a *Sermon*, is designed to be studied as well as read. This study is made possible by the advance publication of all the references in the *Christian Science Quarterly*. On the other hand, the references used at the Wednesday meetings, however carefully prepared, are not published, and are intended to be heard by the attendants at those meetings, but not to be studied in advance. They may well bring out a clear and specific *lesson*—although not in the same sense as the selections chosen to form the Lesson-Sermon, from which they are completely distinct.

The preparation of the readings used at the Wednesday meet-

ings provides the alert First Reader with a welcome opportunity
and responsibility to deal with subjects of timely importance or
special interest in the community, in addition to laying stress
upon countless topics of perennial significance to be found in
both the Bible and *Science and Health*. Mrs. Eddy's provision
that the weekly Lesson-Sermons should be used throughout the
world for unified study, while the Wednesday readings were to
be prepared locally for each individual church, seems to me to
give further indication of her wisdom in providing for both
uniformity and individuality in the denomination she founded.

Therefore, because of the complete freedom of choice in selection of subjects for the Wednesday readings, the First Reader
is at liberty to present helpful and encouraging passages from
the Bible and *Science and Health* in times of distress or emergency, or when the thoughts of the congregation are liable to
be turned towards some current subject or occasion.

Perhaps the public thought has been stirred by some great
fear of a specific type of disaster, epidemic or disease—flood,
influenza, infantile paralysis, heart trouble, or the like. What an
opportunity exists for the Reader to present a series of prayerfully selected passages from the Bible and the Christian Science
textbook, providing support and encouragement, and in many
cases, specific instances of the overcoming of the very problems
in question through trust in and understanding of the law of
God.

Election Day may well suggest readings concerning the spiritual government of the one divine Mind, God; Armistice Day, a
reminder of the Biblical assurances of peace, and Mrs. Eddy's
confirmation of them; Independence Day, the emphasis on man's
true freedom when subject to the law of divine Principle!

Thus, while the First Reader in a Christian Science church
is expected to provide approximately 150 Wednesday readings
during the three year term of office, he can draw upon a vast
variety of material in his two great source books, because of the

breadth, depth and purity of their statement of the infinite Principle, God.

My own experience has been that if the selections are so chosen that the subject is clearly defined, showing both continuity and logical development (as, for that matter, in any type of speaking or writing) the thought which the Reader seeks to convey is more easily grasped and more readily retained by the congregation, and the readings serve as a preparation for the direct part in the meeting which falls to the listeners, and will be described in a moment. It is usual for the message of the hymns to fit in with the subject of the readings.

Immediately following the selections read by the First Reader, we pause for a brief period of Silent Prayer, followed by the reverent repetition of the Lord's Prayer by the congregation led by the Reader. After singing another hymn from our Hymnal, we come to what is perhaps the most characteristic part of our Wednesday meetings—the spontaneous and unrehearsed sharing of thoughts concerning Christian Science, and more especially the relating of experiences indicating its efficacy in bringing inspiration and in overcoming sickness, inharmony, lack, and problems of all kinds.

Actually, our Wednesday meetings are essentially cooperative in nature, for even allowing for the time devoted to hymns, prayer and the selections read by the First Reader, approximately half the time allotted for the meeting is directly in the hands of the congregation.

As might be expected, there is wide variation not only in what is said, but in how it is expressed. Some speak quietly and even haltingly, others clearly and with well modulated tones. Some may say only a few brief words of gratitude, while others tell at some length of what Christian Science has done for them. But over a period of years, and in attending many Christian Science churches in this country and abroad, I have always been impressed by the one common denominator of those who testify on such occasions.

It must surely be evident even to the visitor who knows little or nothing of Christian Science that sincere gratitude is uppermost in the thoughts of those who speak. For some who may be shy by nature, it often constitutes a real victory to be able to stand up and tell what good Christian Science has brought into their experience, however timidly or briefly they may express themselves. Their eagerness to share their experience with others who may be helped and encouraged by it, often aids in overcoming a sense of diffidence or of personal inadequacy.

The spontaneity and wide variety of such testimonies adds to their interest, especially, perhaps, when the speaker outlines simply the thoughts or passages which were of special help to him in the experience which he recounts.

In many cases, the speakers tell of the overcoming of specific instances of sickness, disease or accident in their own experience, but the visitor will soon discover that, important and widespread as such healings are among earnest students of Christian Science, this Science is equally effective in working out problems of lack, inharmonious business or family relationships, of loss, unemployment, and so forth—to mention only a few of the areas in which they are helped by prayerful study of the writings of Mary Baker Eddy in the light of the Bible.

Frequently a speaker will tell of a healing which he had witnessed or experienced before becoming an active student, and which had helped to open his eyes to the healing effects of Christian Science treatment. Many tell with deep gratitude of how this Science and its interpretation of the Bible, have brought to them a fuller understanding of the true nature of God, and a clearer recognition of what it means to be a child of God, as the Bible teaches. Still others relate how through their study of this great subject, new light has been cast for them upon Scriptural passages which had previously seemed obscure. Then many explain how prejudices, or other mental attitudes such as stubbornness, jealousy, envy, resentment, fear, anxiety, have gradually or swiftly disappeared as a result of their consistent study of Christian Science. Others will speak of their deep gratitude for the preventive and protective aspects of this healing truth.

In fact, so varied are the statements made by individuals at these Wednesday meetings held throughout the world, that to attempt to indicate specifically the categories into which they may be said to fall, might well be misleading. However, when we realize that Christian Science is not merely a religion but a way of life, applicable to every aspect of human experience, it can readily be seen that the scope of what is said by the speakers at such meetings is equally wide.

I should like to re-emphasize that what is said by those who speak during the period set apart for the recounting of testimonies of healing and other remarks concerning Christian Science and its practical application is completely unrehearsed. Neither the other members of the congregation, nor the First Reader who conducts the meeting, have any means of knowing (still less of arranging) who the speakers will be, or what they are going to say. Whoever wishes to speak simply rises, is recognized by the First Reader, who acts as Moderator, and when that speaker concludes his remarks, the process is repeated. The timing of any given testimony is left to the individual and to the discretion of the First Reader.

The thought in general is that this part of the Wednesday meeting in a Christian Science church belongs to and is the joyous responsibility of the congregation, the only limits being those of propriety and courtesy, as at any well-conducted meeting.

When the time set aside for individual speakers has ended, the Reader announces a final hymn, in which all take part.

There is no formal Benediction at the close of this meeting, but it may be added that most, and it is to be hoped all, of those who attend have already received a blessing, as a result of the hymns, readings and prayer—and especially, perhaps, from the individual reports of *healing* in its widest sense, shared by those who have taken part.

In our *Church Manual* provision is made for an annual *Thanksgiving Day service,* which in the United States is always held on a Thursday late in November, officially designated as Thanksgiving Day. In other countries, if no such specific day is set apart, it is customary for Christian Scientists to hold this special service on some other suitable occasion, such as New Year's Day.

The basic elements of our Thanksgiving service are similar to those found in our Sunday services, but it has certain distinctive characteristics in keeping with the thought of the day.

After an opening hymn, our Order of Service calls for the reading of the Thanksgiving Proclamation of the President of the United States, or of the Governor of the state in which the service is being held, or both. Then comes the reading of an appropriate selection from the Scriptures, silent prayer and the audible repetition of the Lord's Prayer, with its spiritual interpretation—which has already been mentioned—and an additional hymn.

The Lesson-Sermon which follows at this point differs from any of those used at our Sunday services, in that it is somewhat shorter, while its theme is specifically "Thanksgiving"—although it is prepared for publication in the *Christian Science Quarterly* by the same committee designated to provide the Sunday Lesson-Sermons.

Because of the perennial gratitude felt by students of Christian Science for the goodness and power of God as proved in their daily experience, every service or meeting we hold has the underlying thought of thanksgiving, but the lesson on this joyous day lays special stress upon it; while the solo is usually in the same vein.

The Thanksgiving Day service is also reminiscent of our Wednesday testimony meetings, for after the solo an opportunity is provided for those who wish to do so, to testify briefly to their deep gratitude for individual benefits received as a consequence of their study and application of Christian Science. We feel it to be a truly happy occasion, the more so, as I see it, because usually so many children are present with their parents and join in the Thanksgiving hymns, and sometimes in the testimonies.

Following a further hymn from the Christian Science Hymnal, the service concludes exactly as on Sundays, with the reading of the scientific statement of being, from the Christian Science textbook, and its correlative Scripture from I John 3:1-3, and a suitable Benediction.

FIVE

CHRISTIAN SCIENCE
AND THE SACRAMENTS

WHILE acknowledging and respecting the sincerity and devotion of other Christian denominations in their interpretation of the sacraments of Baptism and Communion and the rites or ceremonies so consistently attached to them, Christian Scientists feel, as did their Leader, Mrs. Eddy, that their approach to these sacraments, while different in some respects from that of others, reflects the spirit and fulfills the meaning of the Master's teaching.

Presumably all thoughtful Christians would agree that the central point in both Baptism and Communion is to be found in their basic spiritual meaning and intent, no matter how dignified and beautiful the ceremonial observances associated with them may be. For example, echoing the phraseology of the Westminster Larger Catechism, my father, an ordained minister of the Church of Scotland in which I received my early training, used often to speak of baptism as "an outward sign of an inward and spiritual grace."

Whether the rite of baptism with water be performed in infancy, or, as some churches practice it, in more mature years when it is a matter of choice and decision on the part of the

84

one who thus approaches church membership, it is surely considered as symbolic of the purification or cleansing associated with the acceptance of the duties of Christian living, whether by the one being baptized, or in the case of a child, by his parents or godparents on his behalf.

Christian Scientists view baptism in the light of an ever-renewed process of cleansing, both of thought and practice, not limited in time or intent to any specific act or ceremony. They consider it as constituting a daily challenge to purity of living, and as a consecration of motives and ideals to the service of God, in obedience to the example and commands of the first Christian. While we do not have a rite of baptism in the sense of immersion in or sprinkling with water, baptism remains to us a real, living and continuous act, a practical manifestation of the way of life to which we are committed.

The breadth and scope of this concept of baptism has brought deep inspiration to the members of our church, and we feel that far from conflicting with Christ Jesus' teaching and practice, as we understand them, it confirms his thought and plan.

There is no doubt that, as the Gospels bring out, Jesus commended and indeed commanded baptism, but we understand his words to have primary reference to the mental purification involved, rather than to an outward act or ceremony. In a significant passage, the writer of the Fourth Gospel appears to indicate that in so far as any physical rite was concerned, the Master left it to his disciples. "Jesus himself did not baptize," John tells us, contradicting a rumor which had reached the Pharisees, "but only his disciples." (John 4:2—*Revised Standard Version*.)

It is equally clear, however, that the Master himself was baptized by John the Baptist in a literal sense, in accordance with a Jewish practice already familiar before his ministry began, but it is significant that he explained his submission to this rite as a concession to a popular religious custom of the day: "Suffer it to be so now: for thus it becometh us to fulfil all righteousness" (or "all pious observance," as it may also be translated.) The real

significance of this event surely lies in the descent upon him of
the Spirit of God, and the reassurance of his divine sonship.

That the Baptist himself had a clear realization of the contrast
between the baptism with water which he practiced and a more
spiritual type of baptism which he associated with the Messiah,
Christ Jesus, is shown in the following verses: "And John bore
witness, 'I saw the Spirit descend as a dove from heaven, and it
remained on him. I myself did not know him; but he who sent
me to baptize with water said to me, 'He on whom you see the
Spirit descend and remain, this is he who baptizes with the Holy
Spirit.' " (John 1:32, 33—R.S.V.) Matthew's record adds: "He
will baptize you with the Holy Spirit and with fire." (Matt. 3:11
—R.S.V.)

Christian Scientists understand Matthew's prediction in terms
of spiritual purification, combined with the destruction of error,
while with many other Christians, we are inclined to associate
this fiery baptism, practiced by Christ Jesus himself, with the
testing of motive and character, in accord with the familiar idiom
of testing or assaying metals to assure their standard of quality
or to separate them from the dross or rough ore in which so
many of them are found in their natural state.

In considering the question of the meaning and practice of
baptism, it is interesting to note that the Apostle Paul, who
again and again lays stress upon the importance of purity and
purification in his writings, apparently felt that according to
his understanding of the teachings of the Master he was not
expected to baptize extensively in any literal sense of the term.
"Christ," he writes, "sent me not to baptize, but to preach the
gospel." (I Cor. 1:17)

In their search for God and an ever deeper understanding
of Him, Christian Scientists recall Jesus' assurance in the Beatitudes that inward purity of thought leads the way to a clearer
vision of Deity. Then, too, bearing in mind the deep significance
attached to the word "name," especially in the writings of the
Old Testament, as indicating again and again the "character"

of the individual, baptism in, or into, the *name* of the Lord may well indicate the progressive acceptance of or approximation to the character of God Himself, in whose image and likeness all were created, according to the spiritual record of creation in the first chapter of Genesis. The mental and spiritual cleansing necessarily involved in any approach to such a high standard, surely has a part in fulfilling the intent of baptism.

Seeing in baptism, as we understand and seek to practice it, an act or process of inward purification, associated with heart-felt repentance and seasoned with selfless love, it holds for us a depth of meaning which cannot but have an abiding effect upon our lives. Instead of being a solemn rite administered from without and on a specific day, baptism is to us an equally solemn, but also constant and consistent challenge to spiritual renewal and cleansing, to the progressive overcoming of sin or error in their many and varied forms and disguises.

To all Christian Scientists, *Communion*—in thought and in practice—possesses a deep and abiding significance, but, as in the case of baptism, we seek to attain to the *spiritual* meaning of the Eucharist, dispensing with the literal use of sacramental bread and wine, as we dispense with the use of actual baptismal water. This in no way lessens the sincerity and solemnity of our approach to God; nor does it run counter to our understanding of the words and acts of the Master Christian.

Every student of the Gospels is familiar with the vivid and poignant events of the Last Supper, but may it not be that many, focussing their attention on every detail of that momentous meeting on the very eve of Jesus' crucifixion, tend to forget momentarily some of the deeply spiritual teaching which he gave to his followers on other occasions during his ministry?

On the face of it, it might appear, especially perhaps from the tradition recorded by St. Paul, who, of course, was not personally present, that Jesus had indeed instituted a continuing ceremony based on the use of bread and wine in the literal sense, no matter how sincere and spiritual the thought of the communicants might be. Mary Baker Eddy, and those of us who have carefully studied and thoughtfully accepted her teachings, find in an equally thorough study of the Gospels, evidence indicating the metaphorical and spiritual sense in which Christ Jesus himself repeatedly used the key terms associated with the Last Supper as the accounts of it have come down to us.

What may seem like a relatively minor point, but one which stands out clearly in my recollection of my earliest studies of "Communion" as understood in Christian Science, is Mrs. Eddy's interpretation of the Master's breaking of bread in the sense of explaining or imparting the Truth to his followers. I was of course familiar with the idiomatic use of the verb in such a phrase as 'breaking the news' to someone, but it had never before occurred to me that it could logically be applied in the context of the Lord's Supper, thereby clarifying a phrase which I had always assumed must be taken literally, and leading directly to my acceptance of the explanation of this momentous event which Christian Science offers.

This paragraph, which is headed "Heavenly supplies," follows a description of Jesus' meeting with the apostles in the upper room at Jerusalem, and reads as follows (*Science and Health:* p. 33): "His followers, sorrowful and silent, anticipating the hour of their Master's betrayal, partook of the heavenly manna, which of old had fed in the wilderness the persecuted followers of Truth. Their bread indeed came down from heaven. It was the great truth of spiritual being, healing the sick and casting out error. Their Master had explained it all before, and now this bread was feeding and sustaining them. They had borne this bread from house to house, *breaking* (explaining) it to others, and now it comforted themselves."

It is of interest to note that it is St. Paul alone, among the New Testament writers describing the events of the Last Supper who speaks of the stern condemnation awaiting whoever "eateth and drinketh unworthily . . . not discerning the Lord's body."

(I Cor. 11:29) The apostle's words have generally been understood as emphasizing the need of prayer and self-examination before partaking of bread and wine in memory of the Master, but may it not be that he was warning his readers of the danger of not discerning what Christ Jesus meant by his *body,* and by the *bread* which he spoke of in the same breath? In the following chapter of the same epistle, Paul would have his Corinthian converts remember that they "are the body of Christ"—if you will, the practical embodiment of the ideas taught and practiced by the first Christian.

As "the living bread which came down from heaven," and moreover as "the way, the truth, and the life"—to use descriptions directly applied to himself by Christ Jesus—he provided the spiritual sustenance which his followers needed to support their growing faith and understanding, the truth which they required to assure their stability and impel their progress.

It will be recalled that another familiar illustration which Jesus used in instructing his disciples was that of the vine and its branches—branches which were fruitful as long as they remained parts of the main stem, but quickly withered when detached from it. Speaking of himself as "the true vine," he made it plain that unless his followers kept their contact with him and with his abiding spiritual teaching, they too, like the tendrils of a vine separated from the parent stem, would quickly wither— they would fail in their efforts to carry on fruitful activity and to inspire others, as the faded branches produced no grapes and consequently no wine.

Thus it was but natural that the Master's words following his Passover meal with his disciples should make use of familiar Gospel metaphors concerning bread, vineyards and wine, with their implications of spiritual nourishment, activity and inspiration, in preparing his followers to take their stand and to carry on the great mission which he expected them to perform when he was no longer personally present to act as their leader and their guide.

It is, then, in this symbolic sense, repeatedly employed in the Master's illustrations, that Christian Scientists understand his inspiring words and seek daily to accept the challenge of active participation in the work he did and urged his followers to do—the opportunity which he afforded to his disciples in all ages to gain more of the character which he exemplified and which he would have them claim and manifest as children of God.

Turning once again to the records of the Last Supper, we find various references to "the cup" and to the fact that the Master called upon all his disciples to drink from it. On the assumption that Jesus had been speaking of *bread* in a literal sense, it is not unnatural that many should regard the *cup* as a cup of wine; but bearing in mind the wider context of his spiritual teaching, Christian Scientists point to Jesus' words in the garden of Gethsemane—words apparently uttered only a few hours later—when he prayed that the bitter cup of impending suffering and trial might be taken from his lips, while still remaining humbly willing to drink it, if this formed part of the divine plan of salvation for all. To us, then, the drinking of the Master's cup implies willingness to accept as he did without flinching the difficulties, oppositions, trials such as often face any who seek consistently to follow the steep and narrow path of spiritual progress.

Further statements in the various accounts of the Last Supper, associating bread and wine with the body and blood of Christ Jesus, seem to have confused the issue for many. I have found it illuminating to view such phraseology in the light of Jesus' words on another occasion, when he affirmed "He that eateth my flesh, and drinketh my blood, dwelleth in me, and I in him." (John 6:56) In this verse the Master appears to me to indicate that such a relationship of indwelling and mutual understanding is so intimate that it might be viewed as the equivalent of assimilating his very flesh and blood.

Granted then that Christian Scientists do not literally eat bread and drink wine in memory of Christ Jesus, they seek to put into practice the spiritual meaning which, according to their understanding, the Master attached to such terms. The Communion or Sacrament services held twice a year in all branch churches of our denomination are not distinguished by any ritual act, but they do include a period devoted to silent individual communion with God—the one God of the universe—during which we seek to realize more fully our union and spiritual relationship with Him, with a view to becoming better Christians—and Christian Scientists.

Since no special rite is involved in connection with our concept of communion, it is our effort to make our communion with Deity a daily experience. Just as in the case of baptism, we view it as a continuing process of conscious purification of thought and life. Hence it must certainly be seen that Christian Scientists have neither eliminated nor ignored baptism or communion, but constantly seek to gain and apply their true meaning in individual experience.

The Mother Church of our denomination in Boston, while using semi-annually the same Lesson-Sermon on "Sacrament" as its branches, omits the special period set aside for personal communion observance. Lest the communion service lose its deeper significance and take on the character of a mere pilgrimage for the occasion and a friendly meeting of its widely scattered members, Mrs. Eddy abolished the communion observance in The Mother Church, while allowing it to remain in the branch churches, many of which were eager to retain it. Even fifty years ago, when this rule became effective, The Mother Church had already some 48,000 members in all parts of the world, while its main edifice seated only about five thousand. Thus obviously only a small proportion could have attended such a special service, as was pointed out at the time.

The reader will recall that, following his resurrection, the Master greeted his disciples in the light of early dawn, just as they brought their fishing boats to land after a long night of unsuccessful toil. As so often before, he brought them encourage-

ment and hope, not merely providing the fish they lacked, but
also proving anew by his presence in their midst that he had
indeed risen from the dead.

It must have been a truly joyous occasion when he and his
followers ate together on the shore of the lake which had witnessed so many instances of the good Physician's healing work,
not to mention his demonstration of power over the elements,
and of his overcoming of lack. Was it not, moreover, a meeting
of deeply spiritual import? At least it is in this light that it is
regarded by Christian Scientists, who have this simple, but
highly significant meal in thought, when they, like the disciples
of old, seek reverently to commune with God and to partake of
the Truth offered by His beloved Son.

In a few brief but vivid sentences (*Science and Health:* p. 35),
the Discoverer and Founder of Christian Science brings into
focus our understanding of the intent of the Master's exhortation
to his disciples on the very eve of his betrayal, trial, and crucifixion, which were shortly to be followed by the joyous events
of his resurrection and ascension, and I quote them here as
providing a fitting conclusion to this chapter. "Our Eucharist
is spiritual communion with the one God. Our bread, 'which
cometh down from heaven,' is Truth. Our cup is the cross. Our
wine the inspiration of Love, the draught our Master drank
and commended to his followers."

SIX

DOES THE CHRISTIAN SCIENCE CHURCH HAVE A CREED?

I N MANY, and perhaps most Christian churches, great stress
is laid on the traditional creeds of Christendom, notably on
what is commonly called *The Apostles' Creed* (although it is generally considered to date from considerably after the time of the
original apostles), and on the creed sponsored by the Council of
Nicaea in the fourth century.

My own familiarity with these creeds began at a very early
age. As far back as I can remember, we repeated the Nicene
Creed with my father at family prayers each Sunday morning,
and the Apostles' Creed with the congregation at the church
services which he conducted as a Presbyterian minister. Even
now, there is much in both these familiar confessions of faith
with which I—and I suppose other students of Christian Science
—would wholeheartedly agree, although at the same time they
contain points which we cannot conscientiously accept, in that
they conflict with our understanding of the teachings of the
Bible. A further reason why Christian Scientists do not use such
creeds in their traditional form lies in the fact that by their very
title, *creeds* imply official statements of belief, while in our
denomination stress is laid on individual understanding rather

than belief, and above all on demonstration—the proving of the practicality of Christ Jesus' words and deeds in present experience. Like the apostle James, we prefer to express by means of action—including healing—the vitality of our faith, proving our acceptance of the Master's teachings and promises by obeying and fulfilling them to the best of our ability.

Before she discovered Christian Science, Mary Baker Eddy herself, as an active member of the Congregational Church, accepted its creed, and although she did not adopt the form of that creed when establishing the church she founded, she never relinquished its inner meaning. (See *Science and Health:* p. 351.)

Throughout her long and productive career, practice invariably took precedence of profession, and being fully aware of the inclination of many to accept either a dogma or a creed in a literal or even stereotyped fashion—without pausing, as she did, to assess and gain its deeper spiritual meaning—she saw the wisdom of turning away from verbal creeds. This in no way implies that Christian Scientists do not accept the fundamentals of Christian faith as set forth in the Bible and primarily, of course, in the New Testament. Moreover, as I see it, the fact that they do not have a *creed,* in the generally accepted sense, indicates not so much criticism of, or divergence from the substance of the orthodox creeds of Christendom, but rather a difference of approach.

Making use of the same basic Scriptural source book appealed to by those who developed the Apostles', the Nicene, and other well known Christian creeds, Mary Baker Eddy recorded clearly in her textbook the fundamental points of Christianity as they were revealed to her. However, instead of formulating them as articles of faith—such as are found in the creeds—she set them forth as tenets, points firmly held by herself and by her church, viewing them in terms of acknowledgment or acceptance rather than of belief.

However exalted and sincere may be the statements of faith or belief in any of the creeds, even those most widely known—

as I have studied them—provide no direct indication on the part of the believer of his preparedness to put his beliefs into actual practice. Granted that this may be due in part to the very form in which most creeds appear, with their repetition of the introductory phrase "I believe. . . . ," the fact remains that they contain no explicit promise to implement, in so far as this is humanly possible, what has been stated.

By way of contrast, it may interest the reader to know that before becoming a member of our denomination, the applicant is called upon to subscribe not only to the fundamental points which we hold or accept, but also to a solemn pledge with which they conclude, to obey certain Biblical rules of far-reaching import which, if universally accepted, might well usher in the millennium. True, the Scriptural rules embodied in this pledge are presumably familiar to every careful student of the Bible, but the significant fact remains that not only are they combined, but also that Christian Scientists enter into a specific contract to obey them to the highest of their understanding.

As one might expect, they include acceptance of the Golden Rule. We also dedicate ourselves to practice mercy, justice and purity, and to accept the government of the one divine Mind, God, which, as St. Paul declared "was also in Christ Jesus"; and to exercise that alert watchfulness and prayer which the Master himself enjoined on his disciples on the night before his crucifixion.

As individuals, we do not claim to have reached the summit of our aspirations in these respects, but the very consistency and earnestness of our efforts to attain progressively to an ever more enlightened understanding of and love for God, and our fellow men, and to conform our character and practice to such rules as these, is surely an augury presaging our eventual success.

The familiar "Apostles' Creed" begins, of course, with the words "I believe in God. . . .", and while that specific phrase is not often found in the writings of Mary Baker Eddy, or on the lips of Christian Scientists, their full acceptance of the power, presence and glory of God is beyond question. Moreover they joyously acknowledge the supremacy and infinity of Deity, giving to Him the adoration which is His due. In fact, Mrs. Eddy's concept of God, based on her long and faithful study of the Scriptures, was so exalted that she could not accept the divided authority which she felt to be implied in the orthodox doctrine of the Trinity, with its assumption of three persons in one Godhead. In short, she concurred with the inspired pronouncement recorded in the book of Deuteronomy: "Hear, O Israel: The LORD our God is one LORD."

With sincere Christians of other denominations, as with the members of the Jewish faith, Christian Scientists accept but one God, whose authority and government, whose loving care and limitless creative activity are undivided and unchallenged, and we feel that in the Bible itself we have ample authority for so doing.

It will be recalled that Christ Jesus expressly distinguished himself from God when he refused to be hailed as "Good Master" on the ground that One alone could lay claim to the designation of "good" in the absolute sense of the term, and that One was God Himself. "There is none good but one, that is, God." (Matt. 19:17)

In this connection it may be stated that Christian Scientists fully accept Christ as the Son of God, the supreme manifestation of the eternal Christ-idea, and are assured that Christ Jesus' individual mission has never been and could never be supplanted or repeated. This does not mean, however, that we affirm the deity of Jesus, for to do so would be to run counter to his own words. Yet this in no way lessens our complete acceptance of and deep and daily gratitude for his marvellous teachings and example, and for the salvation from all ills—mental, moral and physical—which he offered to all mankind.

Christian Science, then, draws a significant distinction between Jesus and the Christ—a distinction which again finds cogent support in the Biblical records. *Jesus,* as is well known, was a proper name rather widely used in Bible times, being the Greek form of the Hebrew Joshua—both signifying "saviour."

It will be remembered that *Christ,* on the other hand, derived from the Greek *Christos,* is identical in meaning with the Hebrew *Mashiach* (or Messiah)—both having the literal sense of "anointed" or "consecrated."

We join with other Christians in maintaining that Jesus, the son of the virgin mother, brought fulfillment to the prophetic ideal of Messiahship, and was consecrated by God Himself for the performance of his unique mission of enlightenment, healing and salvation.

Jesus, then, as I understand the Bible and the writings of Mary Baker Eddy based thereon, was human, in that he had a human mother and walked as a man among men, in spite of his unrivalled understanding of Deity; while the Christ might almost be said to indicate the nature and content of his Messianic assignment, implying the peculiar intimacy of his relationship to God—the divinity which clearly governed his every thought and act.

Does not this correspond closely to the thought brought out by that great expounder of the Christian faith, St. Paul, who clearly distinguished the Master from God, while at the same time setting forth Jesus, the Christ, as the ideal interpreter of God to men? For in instructing his young disciple Timothy, Paul writes: "There is one God, and one mediator between God and men, the man Christ Jesus." (I Tim. 2:5)

In the orthodox creeds, it is customary for a statement of belief in the Holy Ghost to follow after the assertion of faith in God and in His Son, Jesus Christ, and without question the deep significance of the Holy Ghost or Holy Spirit, whom the Master also named the Comforter (John 14:26), is reverently acknowledged by the members of our church.

The Biblical concept of the Comforter is a broad and interesting one, which obviously cannot be discussed in detail here, although a thorough study of the Bible references combined with the writings of Mary Baker Eddy on this subject will be found most rewarding. From one viewpoint, as just noted, Jesus could identify the Comforter with the Holy Ghost, while from another, his close friend and associate John, could see Jesus as himself fulfilling the role of Comforter through the expression of the eternal Christ, Truth—for the term translated "advocate" in the King James Version of I John 2:1 (*parakletos*) is in most other passages rendered as "Comforter." "If any man sin, we have an *advocate* [comforter] with the Father, Jesus Christ the righteous."

One of the most interesting and provocative passages in the New Testament referring to the Comforter is that in which the Master, while in no way deprecating or minimizing his own mission of comfort and of healing, reassures and encourages his followers by promising them that when he is no longer with them in person, God will provide for them, in answer to his prayers, *another* Comforter to be their constant guide. (John 14:16)

As might be expected, much thought has been given through the centuries by theologians and others to the question of the nature and practical effects of this "Spirit of truth" to be imparted by our heavenly Father, as predicted by Christ Jesus. Mary Baker Eddy understood the Master's promise as having its fulfillment in *Divine Science,* a phrase which she sometimes uses to indicate the transcendent heights and depths of her great discovery, which were put into practical effect in human affairs through Christian Science.

Bearing in mind the breadth of the Biblical concept of the Comforter, variously identified as the Spirit of truth and as the Holy Ghost, while also considered as including an important aspect of the mission of the Christ, Christian Scientists feel justified in regarding their faith, in its fullest significance as providing the answer to the Master's promise regarding the coming to humanity of yet "another Comforter."

In support of this we point to countless practical evidences of sin reformed, sickness healed, limitation of all kinds banished, through a growing understanding of God, as revealed to Mary Baker Eddy, and in fulfillment of Christ Jesus' loving but urgent demands upon his followers in all ages, that they could and should carry on his healing work and even expand its effects. "He that believeth on me," declared the first Christian, "the works that I do shall he do also; and greater works than these shall he do; because I go unto my Father." (John 14:12)

The concept of the Trinity held by Mary Baker Eddy is developed in various passages in her writings, including the following, which, as I see it, indicates with peculiar clarity her understanding and appreciation of this great Christian fact. Under the paragraph heading "Divine trinity" she writes (*Science and Health:* pp. 331-332):—"Life, Truth, and Love constitute the triune Person called God,—that is, the triply divine Principle, Love. They represent a trinity in unity, three in one, —the same in essence, though multiform in office: God the Father-Mother; Christ the spiritual idea of sonship; divine Science or the Holy Comforter. These three express in divine Science the threefold, essential nature of the infinite. They also indicate the divine Principle of scientific being, the intelligent relation of God to man and the universe."

A consistent acceptance of this relationship between God and man taught in the first chapter of Genesis, with its insistence that man is indeed none other than the image and likeness of Deity, and continued throughout the Scriptures, with their emphasis on God's parenthood and man's sonship, is of the very essence of our faith.

As will be seen later, it is largely on this basis that Christian Science healing is brought about—healing which does not, as we see it, involve any real change from imperfection to perfection, or from sickness to health, but rather an awakening, a dawning recognition of the fact that nothing has ever happened, or could ever happen, to deface or even to dim God's image and likeness.

One of the clauses in the Apostles' Creed affirms belief in "the forgiveness of sins," and while the fact of divine forgiveness is likewise stressed in Christian Science, it is viewed by our church as implying much more than unconditional pardon. Such pardon of itself might well open the way to further sinning, if it were not contingent upon divinely-aided repentance and reform, which in turn bring about the overcoming and eventual destruction of sin.

Cannot the very nature of God be viewed as destroying sin, by its sublime perfection, as surely as light banishes darkness, and as even human love, reflecting the Love which is God, quickly learns to overcome hate? It will be recalled that when Christ Jesus—who so fully understood the nature of his heavenly Father—forgave a woman accused of flagrantly violating the Seventh Commandment, he made this searching, but constructive demand of her, that she "go, and sin no more."

Divine forgiveness, as we understand it, is further viewed as implying or imparting a growing understanding of God, which enables man to see that sin shares the ultimate unreality and powerlessness which we also associate with sickness, thereby overcoming it progressively in ourselves—and in others when called upon for help. On the other hand, however unreal sin may be in the final analysis, we maintain that it remains real to *us*, as long as we believe in it, and that it will be punished so long as we insist on making it real in our experience by indulging in it.

Without doubt every Christian denomination has its individual teaching or interpretation regarding the great subject of Atonement; in fact I still recall vividly the hours I spent as a theological student in attempting to master the numerous and often conflicting concepts of atonement which were presented to us. Not only so, but my class notes lie before me as I write. From them I confirm my recollection that we were called upon to study and to memorize many separate explanations of atonement —including the Forensic theory, the Military theory, the Debtor theory, the Pedagogic theory, the Therapeutic theory, and so on—together with the points for and against each one.

We studied faithfully the views of Origen and of Gregory of Nyssa, of Athanasius and Anselm, of Irenaeus and Abelard, together with those of divines and philosophers of our own day. We had a fine teacher, one of the most respected theologians of his time, who did his best to guide his students through this maze of conflicting interpretations, but, frankly, it was difficult to escape a sense of confusion.

All these theories of atonement, however, despite their differences and complexities served to emphasize the importance of the theme, indicating that while those who set them forth might not agree regarding the specific *nature* of atonement, at least they uniformly considered it as a *fact* of deep and abiding significance. In view of this, it was but natural that I should continue to explore the subject with the desire to reach some concept of atonement which would be acceptable to me as an individual.

At this point I had no knowledge of the views of the Christian Science Church regarding this great subject, but when in due course, I was introduced to *Science and Health* and undertook to study it in conjunction with the other writings of Mary Baker Eddy—and, of course, in the light of the Bible—I quickly found many passages clarifying the intent of the Scriptural statements, and setting forth what I feel to be the real essence of atonement. For example, the Lesson-Sermon entitled "Doctrine of Atonement" as studied by all Christian Scientists for two weeks out of each year, provides a beautifully developed explanation of this subject.

It is obviously not practical for me to attempt to discuss atonement in any detail here, but I feel that it will be of interest to the reader if I outline a few points which immediately appealed to me, and which have led me to accept as my own the concept of atonement presented by Christian Science.

"Atonement" has so long been viewed as almost exclusively a theological dogma, that in many instances its simple and literal

meaning of *"at-one-ment,"* the state of being at-one or becoming
at-one with God, has been neglected. However, this is perhaps
the primary sense in which it is understood in Christian Science.
Christ Jesus' constant at-one-ment with his heavenly Father
which inspired his words and his works during his ministry,
and which surely contributed to his ability to rise from the grave,
is viewed as a glorious challenge to be accepted progressively by
all on the basis of his example.

How strong was the Master's sense of his own unity with God,
and how clear his eagerness that such unity of thought might be
shared by his disciples, and indeed by all God's children, is indicated in many gospel verses, notably in the 17th chapter of John,
in the course of which Christ Jesus offers this familiar and
memorable prayer on behalf of his followers in all ages, "that
they all may be one; as thou, Father, art in me, and I in thee,
that they also may be one in us..."

This great theme of at-one-ment is surely one of the fundamental contributions of Jesus the Christ to the salvation of
mankind, and above all to the understanding of the nature and
power of God as Love itself.

In addition to its emphasis on union with God, as taught and
proved by the Master, the "Doctrine of Atonement" as we understand it stresses the infinite power of divine Love, God, thereby
lifting thought above and beyond the sad event of the crucifixion, on which so much stress is laid in other views of atonement. True, the crucifixion, with all that it implies of the
Saviour's willingness and readiness to experience death itself
for his convictions and to exhibit the ultimate in self-sacrifice,
was undoubtedly a basic element in his life-long manifestation
of atonement, but, as I understand it, Christian Science with its
stress on God as Life itself, and on the overcoming of death,
rightly reminds us of the triumphant results of this atonement
in the resurrection and ascension.

It may be added that the concept of atonement which views

it as purely vicarious, as a type of sacrificial offering from which others are completely spared because of Jesus' personal sacrifice, is not accepted by Christian Science, which stresses the point that, following his example, we are all called upon to do our part, individually, in overcoming sin, although the cost may appear to be great. As I see it, this view in no degree lessens the unique significance of the Saviour's perpetually redemptive and atoning work. Rather does it provide additional evidence of his guidance and leadership in providing an example for all to follow.

The problem presented by the crucifixion may surely be said to have found its solution in the resurrection and in that further advancing stage of progress which we know as the ascension; and this essential sequence proved beyond all cavil the Master's consummate understanding of the power of Life, God. He had raised others from the grave during the period of his ministry. Now he had demonstrated not only for himself, but by himself, that death could not put an end to Life. In his resurrection and ascension, Christ Jesus surely provided the best possible proofs of the practicality of what he taught, by inspiring the faith of his followers to grasp in increasing measure the fact of "eternal life" which he had so constantly emphasized as shown in the Gospel records.

Seeking to pattern their experience on that of the early disciples, Christian Scientists strive consistently to rise out of and beyond mere belief, into such living faith and still further into that understanding which the Master so earnestly desired of his followers.

In concluding this chapter, I feel it will be of interest to the reader if I record in full the six tenets of The Mother Church, written by Mary Baker Eddy, which the members of our denomination affirm and accept in lieu of any formal creed.

Because of the deep importance which the Discoverer of Christian Science attached to them, they are to be found not only in *Science and Health* (p. 497), but also in our *Church Manual* (pages 15 and 16) from which they are here cited:

"TENETS

of The Mother Church
The First Church of Christ, Scientist
"*To be signed by those uniting with The First Church of Christ, Scientist, in Boston, Mass.*

"1. As adherents of Truth, we take the inspired Word of the Bible as our sufficient guide to eternal Life.

"2. We acknowledge and adore one supreme and infinite God. We acknowledge His Son, one Christ; the Holy Ghost or divine Comforter; and man in God's image and likeness.

"3. We acknowledge God's forgiveness of sin in the destruction of sin and the spiritual understanding that casts out evil as unreal. But the belief in sin is punished so long as the belief lasts.

"4. We acknowledge Jesus' atonement as the evidence of divine, efficacious Love, unfolding man's unity with God through Christ Jesus the Way-shower; and we acknowledge that man is saved through Christ, through Truth, Life, and Love as demonstrated by the Galilean Prophet in healing the sick and overcoming sin and death.

"5. We acknowledge that the crucifixion of Jesus and his resurrection served to uplift faith to understand eternal Life, even the allness of Soul, Spirit, and the nothingness of matter.

"6. And we solemnly promise to watch, and pray for that Mind to be in us which was also in Christ Jesus; to do unto others as we would have them do unto us; and to be merciful, just, and pure."

SEVEN

IS MATTER REAL AND SUBSTANTIAL?

THROUGHOUT the ages mankind has earnestly sought to discover the meaning and essence of life, the nature of pure and essential being, the answer to the riddle of the universe. As one might expect, the solutions offered have been many and various. Some have attempted to propound a purely materialistic explanation of the universe and of man himself, virtually assuming that nature was self-evolved and that man was simply a more refined development or result of a physical evolutionary process.

The *élan vital,* or vital force, on which Bergson laid stress seems only to have been a step above the sovereignty of matter. With Descartes and his famous proposition *Cogito ergo sum*—I think, therefore I am—there is at least some reaching out for a mental basis on which to found existence, although it is obviously the human mind, rather than the divine Mind, God, which provides the foundation of his argument.

In particular, the question of the nature of matter and its effects upon mankind is one which has aroused the interest of inquiring thinkers since long before the commencement of our

Christian era. As early as the 4th century B.C., Democritus had his own atomic theory, and others in ancient Greece pondered the nature of matter; while down through the centuries, natural scientists and physicists, philosophers and occasionally theologians, have turned their attention to the subject.

Up until quite recently, such discussions were viewed as largely academic by the average citizen, who in most cases was content to deal with matter as it appeared to be, as a solid mass of material substance, without serious consideration of the fact that matter was coming to be ever more widely viewed as energy or force in perpetual motion. With the advent of the current Atomic Age, however, the thought of matter as solid and static has been rudely shattered in the public imagination by the widespread discussion of atomic energy and of its potentialities either for the advancement or the destruction of civilization. In the sixth decade of the twentieth century, the consideration of the nature of matter is no longer confined to the laboratory of the scientist or to the study of the philosopher. It is a vital issue of our day, concerning every thinking individual.

There are numerous indications which combine to show that Mary Baker Eddy, the Discoverer and Founder of Christian Science, was a woman with a remarkably penetrating and indeed prophetic insight. When she first published her great work *Science and Health with Key to the Scriptures,* little short of a century ago, boldly affirming the power of God, the divine Mind, and the impotence and indeed the complete unreality of matter, matter had not attained to its present prominence as the presumed source of available atomic energy. Yet, even at that time, she saw the wisdom and the necessity of working from the basis of the unlimited power of God to supersede any alleged potentialities of what is commonly called *matter;* while about the turn of the century we find her making this remarkable statement: "Atomic action is Mind, not matter. It is neither the energy of matter, the result of organization, nor the outcome of life infused into matter: it is infinite Spirit, Truth, Life, defiant of error or matter." (*Miscellaneous Writings:* p. 190) Do not these words indicate her assurance that all real power, whether it be termed energy, action or force, finds its source in and derives its control from the one divine Mind, God, and must therefore be as constructive and harmonious as that Mind?

A further indication that Mrs. Eddy foresaw a growing stress upon atomic energy as time went by, is seen in the fact that one of the twenty-six subjects which she selected for the Lesson-Sermons which, as already noted, are studied in rotation by Christian Scientists and read in our churches twice each twelve months, was: "Is the Universe, Including Man, Evolved by Atomic Force?"—and this in the year 1898! A study of her writings indicates unquestionably that she intended this query to be answered in the negative, for she uniformly stressed the creative and maintaining power of God, referring repeatedly to the manifestly spiritual account of creation, as recorded in the opening chapter of Genesis. Moreover Christian Science, as Mrs. Eddy discovered it and set it forth in her textbook, may be said to view evolution not as a material or even semi-material process, but as the creative unfoldment initiated and forever upheld by the one Mind or Spirit, God, who alone governs both man and the universe.

In view of the fact that in our time mankind is constantly assailed by discussions of the nature and all but incalculable effects of atomic and nuclear energy, the amazing timeliness of the Christian Science Lesson-Sermon dealing with this general subject, is beyond dispute.

One of the great and distinctive contributions which Mary Baker Eddy has made to the consideration of the nature of matter is to be found in her oft-repeated conviction to the effect that matter is unreal, untrue, insubstantial, powerless, unintelligent—despite its pretensions to reality, permanence, and unlimited energy. Startling as this assertion has appeared to many, it comes as the natural and indeed inevitable consequence of an unqualified acceptance of the proposition that God is All, completely unbounded and unlimited. Indeed, if God be viewed as all-pervasive divine Mind, or Spirit, how could Deity be logically conceived of as creating or maintaining that which is the very opposite of Himself?

It may be added that this thought of God as *All*—in the absolute sense, to the exclusion of matter—finds a parallel in the book of Isaiah (45:22), for where the Authorized Version reads: "I am God, and there is none" (no one) "else;" the compact Hebrew phrase can be as justly translated, "I am God, and there is *nothing* else;" thereby contributing to the support of Mrs. Eddy's position.

On page 209 of the Christian Science textbook, under the heading *Spiritual translation,* appear these timely and thought-provoking words: "The compounded minerals or aggregated substances composing the earth, the relations which constituent masses hold to each other, the magnitudes, distances, and revolutions of the celestial bodies, are of no real importance, when we remember that they all must give place to the spiritual fact by the translation of man and the universe back into Spirit. In proportion as this is done, man and the universe will be found harmonious and eternal."

If the reader will carefully consider the following reasoning, it should not be difficult to see why the Christian Scientist finds it necessary to divest materiality in all its forms of any claim to man's allegiance. Once the existence of matter has been admitted, how can its inherent material conditions and demands (including disintegration, disease, death) be effectively denied? On the other hand, denying the original claim that matter is real and substantial, rules out completely the nemesis of mortality resulting from any chain reaction of material conditions.

Granted, then, that Christian Science frankly denies the validity of matter's so-called laws and even its very existence as a real entity, it is but natural to ask how it accounts for its apparent reality and substantiality. In all fairness, if such a question be asked of the Discoverer and Founder of *Christian* Science, may it not be asked with equal propriety of the representatives of *natural* science, who, especially in recent years, have increasingly removed from matter its seeming solidity and permanence, resolving it into constantly moving subatomic particles, or into nuclear energy or force.

Microscopic and telescopic examination, electronic analyses, and complex mathematical calculations may lead to this conclusion from the physicist's point of view, but is he not still reasoning from the basic assumption that the universe and man —and energy in all its varied forms—are essentially material? Has any physicist, without appealing to the divine Source of all creation, been able to explain satisfactorily the primary laws and form-giving Cause originating and governing the completely orderly action of the cosmos with which he is concerned, upon which all his calculations and conclusions must depend and without which all would be chaos?

Mary Baker Eddy, on the other hand, reasoning consistently from a wholly spiritual starting point, founded her conclusions on a purely metaphysical platform of the one divine Principle, the one infinite God—Mind, Truth, Life and Love—as the essence, Cause and Creator of all being, including man and the entire universe.

In St. Paul's famous sermon on Mars' Hill, there is clear evidence supporting this same line of reasoning, as his argument builds up to the familiar and triumphant assertion that "God . . . made the world and all things therein," and that "in him we live, and move, and have our being."

Having probed deeply into the nature of what is commonly called matter, Mrs. Eddy saw it as disappearing altogether under the searching and infinitely powerful lens of divine Spirit. She viewed matter as appearance only, as the wrong answer to the problem of existence, and as the alleged counterfeit of God's spiritual ideas.

Being fully aware of the tenacity with which humanity holds to any position or retains any cherished concept, real or illusory, the author of the Christian Science textbook recognized the necessity of vigorously denying the myth of matter, while simultaneously and with equal emphasis affirming the complete authority of Spirit, God.

Knowing also the disastrous results which often accrue when man is suddenly bereft of the comfort of his familiar beliefs and convictions, however erroneous and unsatisfying they may later prove to be, Mary Baker Eddy, throughout her writings, is found providing for the learner support and encouragement, while awakening his thought to spiritual understanding of the power and presence of God.

No better example can be cited to illustrate the deep insight of the Discoverer and Founder of Christian Science and her unmistakable ability not only to transcend human reliance on matter, but also to epitomize the best of the spiritual and philosophical thinking of the ages, than the quotation with which this chapter concludes. For the honest and sincere thinker, this profound declaration written by Mrs. Eddy three quarters of a century ago, will serve to illustrate the irresistible change of emphasis which is already beginning in human thought, and which, once started, can never be turned back.

The efficacy of this carefully worded and deeply spiritual declaration in overcoming sin and disease and in restoring harmony, has been proved in countless instances by students of Christian Science, who constantly affirm it and claim its reality in their own experience. This remarkable statement will be found on page 468 of *Science and Health:*

"*Question.*—What is the scientific statement of being?

"*Answer.*—There is no life, truth, intelligence, nor substance in matter. All is infinite Mind and its infinite manifestation, for

God is All-in-all. Spirit is immortal Truth; matter is mortal error. Spirit is the real and eternal; matter is the unreal and temporal. Spirit is God, and man is His image and likeness. Therefore man is not material; he is spiritual."

EIGHT

WHAT IS CHRISTIAN SCIENCE HEALING?

TO ATTEMPT even to outline an answer to this momentous question within the limits of a single chapter—or even of a single book—is virtually impossible, but some general statements can be made here indicating the breadth and scope of the subject.

Those but slightly acquainted with Christian Science sometimes assume that physical healing is its primary object and result. Actually, as we have seen, this is far from being the case. That Christian Science does indeed bring healing in the limited sense of the word is attested on the basis of many thousands of fully authenticated and permanent cures, but they present but one segment of the circle of harmony maintained by Christian Science.

Students of New Testament Greek will recall that the verb *sozein* means either "to heal" or "to save." Thus *healing*, from the Biblical standpoint, had a much wider purview than is perhaps realized by many conscientious students of the English Bible; and since it is upon the Bible that Christian Science is founded, it is natural and indeed inevitable that it, too, should stress this dual aspect of salvation, which brings relief from both physical and moral infirmity.

Had healing been more widely and actively practiced in the churches of other denominations, it would not perhaps be so

112

specifically associated with Christian Science, and the wider aspects of healing wrought on this basis might have been more clearly seen and more readily appreciated.

Mary Baker Eddy followed the Master himself in recognizing the importance of healing by prayer. His personal practice of such healing, and his repeated injunctions to his followers that they too should carry on this humanitarian work, are clear and unequivocal. Just as he did not stop at that point, but proceeded to deal with the need of overcoming sin, of practicing true brotherhood, of obeying the implications of the commandments, and, from a positive standpoint, the necessity and opportunity of understanding God, so Christian Science never stops with the cure, no matter how welcome to the individual, or spectacular to the bystander, but emphasizes, as Jesus did, the necessity of regeneration.

Doubtless there were many instances, such as the case of the Master's healing of the ten lepers, in which there seemed to be but slight response to his work, for only one returned to express his gratitude; yet we do know from the Gospel record that "the common people heard him gladly," and undoubtedly one reason for this eager acceptance of his message was his readiness and ability to meet their need in terms they could understand.

At the outset of his great career, the Master echoed the words of his forerunner, John, calling upon the people to repent, assuring them of the actual presence of the Kingdom of God. Since the Greek *metanoia,* translated "repentance," meant primarily and literally "change of mind" rather than mere penitence, the Messiah was surely calling upon his countrymen to exhibit a complete change in their thinking, preparatory to the joyous recognition that God's government was not a theoretical possibility, but a present, eternal, and practical reality.

The evidence he presented in justification of his position and authority is summed up in the comprehensive term *healing.* This is brought out with peculiar clarity in the opening chapter of Mark's Gospel, which records three specific cures wrought by Jesus at the commencement of his missionary work, including the over-coming of insanity, fever and even of the dreaded leprosy.

Although leprosy was then considered highly contagious, Jesus did not hesitate to touch the sick man. Evidently his ever-present understanding of the true nature of God and of man assured him that the prevention of disease was as certain as its cure; and so the man was healed, while the Master himself remained un-harmed. This same chapter (verse 34) records that "he healed many that were sick of divers diseases, and cast out many devils."

When John the Baptist became discouraged during his im-prisonment at the hands of Herod and sent word to Jesus asking whether he were indeed the long-awaited Messiah, as John him-self had virtually announced, the answer which he received was unquestionably in the affirmative. Moreover, it is typical of the Master that it was practical, rather than verbal: "Go and shew John again those things which ye do hear and see: The blind receive their sight, and the lame walk, the lepers are cleansed, and the deaf hear, the dead are raised up, and the poor have the gospel preached to them." (Matt. 11:4,5) In short, the validity of Christ Jesus' Messianic claims was firmly established on the basis of the irrefutable efficacy of his works of mercy, in restoring man to the realization of his original sinless state of divinely-bestowed health and well-being.

Later, when his opponents accused him of collaborating with "Beelzebub the chief of the devils," he made it plain that his healing activities in casting out demons (then popularly supposed to cause physical diseases of all kinds) were divinely inspired and proved the presence and power of God's kingdom. "If I with the finger of God cast out devils, no doubt the kingdom of God is come upon you." (Luke 11:20)

Since Christ Jesus attached such vital importance to the work of healing, it comes as no surprise that when twelve of his most consistent disciples were commissioned as *apostles*—messengers or missionaries—one of the primary tasks assigned to them was the healing ministry, and without delay "they departed, and went

through the towns, preaching the gospel, and healing every
where." (Luke 9:6) Christian Scientists not unnaturally ask, "If
this were required of the disciples in those early days, does not
the same demand hold good for Christians of our own day?"—
moreover, we are assured that it does.

Our position in this respect receives express support in the
words of the Master recorded at the close of Mark's Gospel: "Go
ye into all the world, and preach the gospel to every creature. . . .
And these signs shall follow them that believe; In my name shall
they cast out devils; they shall speak with new tongues; They shall
take up serpents; and if they drink any deadly thing, it shall not
hurt them; they shall lay hands on the sick, and they shall re-
cover."

The explicit wording "them that believe" is clearly directed
towards the multitudes in any age and any locality who are ready
and willing to place their uncompromising trust in the same
divine power which Christ Jesus understood and utilized. It is
on this basis that Christian Scientists feel fully justified in claiming, and in an increasing degree experiencing, the results of his
glorious promise.

According to the contemporary accounts of early Christians,
healing the sick and raising the dead by means of prayer, were
widely practiced up to the third century A.D. They seem to have
fallen into disuse as the adherents of Christianity became deeply
involved in ecclesiasticism, largely forgetting the simple and
direct teachings and practice of the great Physician. It would be
interesting to discuss further the reasons for this loss of healing
power, but this is not the place to do so.

A careful study of Christ Jesus' life and work indicates clearly
that his healing activities were of the broadest type, and were
by no means limited to the cure of physical ailments. He was
prepared to meet the needs of those whom he encountered, no
matter what these needs might be. While there were many who
apparently desired physical healing above all else, others were
plagued by moral problems, still others by a condition of lack.

In each case, Jesus dealt with the problem in the form in which it presented itself to the individual.

The "ten lepers" were quickly cured; the man afflicted with "an impediment in his speech" was enabled to express himself clearly; the woman "taken in adultery" won forgiveness on the basis of her repentance; four thousand people were fed promptly and fully from the seemingly meager supplies at hand, in response to the Master's prayer to God; instantly a severe storm abated at Jesus' word—to mention only a few of the proofs he provided of his ever-present understanding of God, and of His law of unlimited good.

Following directly in the footsteps of the Way-shower, Mary Baker Eddy understood and expounded *healing* in the widest sense of that wonderful word. Moreover, she was fully convinced that so far from belonging exclusively to an earlier age, such wonderful works as those associated with Christ Jesus' ministry were possible of accomplishment both here and now. This is clearly shown in her own ringing words as recorded in *Science and Health* (p. 150).

"To-day the healing power of Truth is widely demonstrated as an immanent, eternal Science, instead of a phenomenal exhibition. Its appearing is the coming anew of the gospel of 'on earth peace, good-will toward men.' This coming, as was promised by the Master, is for its establishment as a permanent dispensation among men; but the mission of Christian Science now, as in the time of its earlier demonstration, is not primarily one of physical healing. Now, as then, signs and wonders are wrought in the metaphysical healing of physical disease; but these signs are only to demonstrate its divine origin,—to attest the reality of the higher mission of the Christ-power to take away the sins of the world."

Christian Science, then, as taught by Mrs. Eddy, views *healing* in terms of the 'wholeness' implied in the derivation of the word, showing its applicability to every problem facing the individual or society. Glimpsing progressively the immense possibilities of this new-old religion, directly based on Christ Jesus' words and works and confirmed by the Scriptures as a whole, the Christian Scientist seeks to do his part, not only in accepting its efficacy for himself, but also in proving it for the benefit of others. In so doing, he is convinced that all inharmony stems ultimately from mental rather than physical causes, and that consequently it can only be permanently overcome through the acceptance of the ever-present power of the one divine Mind, God, eternal good.

Convinced that the causes of infection, contagion and disease lie in the human mind and its cherished beliefs, Christian Science proceeds to correct them, not on the basis of psychiatry, suggestion, hypnotism or materia medica, but from the standpoint of specifically Christian healing, with its persistent and unreserved recognition of the ever-loving care and constant support of our heavenly Father, as demonstrated and commended by Christ Jesus.

Like the Master, Christian Science does not countenance the use of drugs, or other material methods of healing. How could any conscientious Christian Scientist, having consistently denied the authority and power of matter, credit it with power to heal? Then, too, if sickness does indeed commence from erroneous thinking, how can any material remedy be considered capable of providing more than limited and temporary relief, and that only to the degree of the patient's faith in the remedy?

Let no one, however, conclude that any Christian Scientist would attempt to infringe upon the rights of his neighbor by depriving him of any material medicament which he may desire, but the fact remains that many individuals eventually abandon such aids of their own accord, and frequently as a direct result of the pronouncement, "There is nothing more that medicine can do for you." Innumerable instances have proved that in Christian Science they find not only healing of the problem in question, but regeneration, together with freedom from countless hindrances to mental and spiritual progress.

A careful examination of the Gospel records suggests that in the course of his great mission of teaching and healing Christ Jesus turned his attention primarily to the destruction of three broad types of human evil, discomfort and disability, commonly known as sin, disease and death. Following the example of their great Way-shower, then, Christian Scientists devote their energies to the task of meeting and overcoming these same problems, realizing that in their wide ramifications they may well be understood as covering evil, error, sickness, lack and inharmony of all kinds—in short, all the ills "that flesh is heir to."

Sin extends far beyond the bounds of a mere moral concept. *Sickness* is by no means restricted to physical disease. *Death* itself is not confined to the conclusion of our mortal sense of existence.

It is, then, to the work of progressively overcoming these three great categories of inharmony that the healing ministry of Christian Science addresses itself. While we have what we call Christian Science practitioners, whose names are listed in The Christian Science Journal, and who devote their full time to this truly humanitarian activity, every sincere student of this subject has his individual part, in greater or lesser degree, in what the Bible calls "the healing of the nations," as well as of individuals.

In short, we maintain that the business man, the housewife, the engineer, the statesman, the lawyer, the soldier—people in all walks of life—can and should, in the course of their daily activities, fulfill the obligations laid upon every Christian Scientist—indeed upon every Christian—by dealing consciously and effectively with sin, sickness, and death, that they may be lessened for all mankind.

The Westminster Shorter Catechism, which I memorized in childhood while attending the Sunday School conducted in my father's church, contains a brief, but remarkably comprehensive definition of *sin:* "Sin is any want of conformity unto, or transgression of, the law of God." The breadth and scope of this definition help to explain why it is that Christian Scientists feel that they have the opportunity of overcoming and destroying sin wherever they may be, whatever they may be doing. If, as the Westminster divines imply, sin is not limited to direct and obvious disobedience to God's law, but includes equally any failure to abide by it in its fullest and widest meaning, then *sin* is much more widespread than one might suppose, and we have to be constantly on the alert to counteract its insidious suggestions. In the words of a familiar hymn (*Christian Science Hymnal;* No. 383):

> "Whatever dims thy sense of truth
>   Or stains thy purity,
>   Though light as breath of summer air,
>   O count it sin to thee."

Any aberration from the straight line of fairness, truth, justice, equity; any compromise with a truly upright standard of conduct or character; any thought which fails to measure up to the implications of the Ten Commandments or the Sermon on the Mount, comes within the meaning of *sin,* as I understand it in the light of Christian Science.

I have long been impressed by the fact that the Hebrew of the Old Testament contains a surprisingly wide range of synonyms for *sin.* The Hebrews viewed it as a heavy burden to be disposed of, and as failure to "hit the mark" of righteousness. They saw it as perversion of the law of God, and negligence in obeying it. It was, to them, rebellion, treachery, transgression against the divine law. Other synonyms indicate clearly their comprehensive concept of sin by showing its results, which included futility, confusion, and finally ruin.

While Christ Jesus obviously did not attribute every disease to sin of some sort, it is significant that throughout the Bible there is repeated evidence of the link between sin, error or evil, and their inharmonious results in the form of illness or disaster for the individual—or, in many instances, on a national scale.

Bearing in mind the variety of the Biblical synonyms for *sin,* and particularly the terms indicating its inherent treachery, futility and confusion, one can readily see the logic of Mary Baker Eddy's words on page 481 of *Science and Health:* "Sin has the elements of self-destruction. It cannot sustain itself. If sin is supported, God must uphold it, and this is impossible, since Truth cannot support error."

This certainly does not mean that Mrs. Eddy ignored, or would have her followers ignore, the manifold and insidious *claims* of sin to both reality and power. She realized that such claims must be combatted by a clear and resolute recognition and unshaken knowledge of the fact that they are indeed illusory, because God, the very essence of good, is supreme.

Only a thorough study of the writings of Mary Baker Eddy will make it possible for the inquirer to gain a correct concept of the Christian Science approach to evil, sin, and materiality in general, and of the methods of healing and reform which the Discoverer of this Science was inspired to set forth. I may add, on the basis of my own experience, that such a study will be found deeply rewarding.

In the progressive overcoming of the many varied aspects of sin, the way is opened for obedience to the Master's command: "Be ye therefore perfect, even as your Father which is in heaven is perfect." Since the Greek term commonly translated "perfect" in this verse also means "complete" or "mature," the gradual approach to and even attainment of such a goal is seen to be within the bounds of possibility, and we may be sure that Christ Jesus would not have required the impossible.

In obeying the Master's further command that Christians should "Heal the sick," and recalling his assurance that such signs or evidences of healing would automatically follow "them that believe," Mary Baker Eddy and her followers have gladly accepted an active part in the healing ministry, and have indeed been forerunners in this new crusade. However, the question is sometimes raised as to their acceptance of another of the Master's commands, that Christians should also "preach the gospel to every creature," when Christian Scientists do not proselytize, nor do they have personal preachers in their churches. Therefore a word of explanation is in order.

"Preaching the Gospel," as we understand it, is of far wider application than "preaching" in the commonly accepted sense. With due respect to the many fine preachers of our own day and of past years, we recall that while the Gospel that Christ Jesus presented to the world undoubtedly contained teaching, exhortation and exposition of Scripture, the records also show that his *words* were constantly accompanied by *works*—by practical, down-to-earth illustrations of what he had to say, in terms of meeting the needs of his audiences.

These illustrations are often termed *miracles,* with the implication that they are inexplicable and therefore miraculous, and that we cannot expect to witness similar events translated into the solution of twentieth-century problems. Christian Science maintains that since God's law necessarily contains the quality of His perfection, so-called *miracles* are simply natural illustrations or proofs of the harmonious operation of that law, and that the imperative needs of men will be met to the extent that they humbly and joyously accept and obey it.

While the most practical and consistent proof of this statement is to be found in the life and work of the Master himself, he did not hesitate to make this startling and emphatic pronouncement: "He that believeth on me, the works that I do shall he do also; and greater works than these shall he do." (John 14:12) Thus it is clear that the Master did not consider his *works* miraculous. To him such activities were natural and inevitable, and were to be expected of those who accepted his teachings and his practice and sought earnestly to emulate his God-bestowed character. That the Christianity which he founded—based more on practice than on doctrine—has within itself that which can meet the needs of mankind in sickness or health, sorrow or joy, want or prosperity, is firmly held by Christian Science.

What more joyous *Gospel* or "good news," what more effective preaching can there be than the assurance and demonstration of the fact that the innumerable problems of mankind, summed up in the words *sin, sickness* and *death,* can be overcome?

Christian Scientists, then, do indeed preach the Gospel; and we honestly feel that we do so in terms of the Master's intention and practice, spreading the good news of healing and salvation, of confident trust and spiritual progress, proving the practicality of our faith by its results.

But what, it may be asked, is the position of Christian Science with regard to that further command of the Master—"Raise the dead"—which is cited on the cover of every copy of *Science and Health?* In what sense do we understand these words and to what extent do we obey them? These challenging questions must surely be faced, not alone by members of our denomination, but by all Christians who are prepared to follow conscientiously Christ Jesus' teachings and practice.

All who accept the accuracy of the Biblical records are aware that the Master restored the dead to life, and further, that prophets in the Old Testament period and apostles in the New, did likewise; and it is clear that Jesus expected such wonderful works of all his followers. My own feeling, as a Christian Scientist, is that so far from being impossible, the overcoming of death is capable of accomplishment in this age, as in earlier ages, on the basis of sufficient consecration, humility and understanding of the permanency of God and of man as His image and likeness. In this connection, however, one significant question would arise: Has the individual given consent to death and would he not, therefore, resist being raised?

In recent years there have appeared in the daily press various accounts of people who have been restored to life after having been pronounced "medically dead." If such case histories be accepted in connection with medical practice, is it not logical and fair to admit the validity of various instances in which individuals who have undergone the experience called *death,* have been restored as the result of Christian Science practice, solely on the basis of consecrated and scientific prayer?

The greatest obstacle to the extension and permanence of such healings lies in the widespread failure to admit their possibility, which St. Paul encountered even in the apostolic age when he asked of King Agrippa: "Why should it be thought a thing incredible with you, that God should raise the dead?" (Acts 26:8)

It is surely significant that in his raising of Lazarus and of Jairus' daughter, the Master, while clearly aware in both instances that the verdict of death had been pronounced upon them, spoke of their condition in terms of sleep, thereby refusing to accept its permanence and finality as outlined by the physical senses. In this connection Mary Baker Eddy writes: "Jesus restored Lazarus by the understanding that Lazarus had never died, not by an admission that his body had died and then lived again. Had Jesus believed that Lazarus had lived or died in his body, the Master would have stood on the same plane of belief as those who buried the body, and he could not have resuscitated it.

"When you can waken yourself or others out of the belief that all must die, you can then exercise Jesus' spiritual power to reproduce the presence of those who have thought they died,—but not otherwise." (*Science and Health:* p. 75)

Granted that individuals may not yet have reached the heights of spiritual understanding required to perform such wonderful works as those accomplished by the Master in raising the dead, instantly stilling the storm, or walking on the water, are we not justified in maintaining that they are still capable of achievement in this age when man is prepared to understand and accept God as Life itself, as truly ever-present and all-powerful?

Surely there is much that can be done by the individual along the way in preparing himself for the overcoming of the "last enemy," which, as Paul confidently affirmed, "shall be destroyed." As I see it, death might almost be considered as the acute stage of a chronic problem, and there is not a little both in the Bible itself and in the writings of Mary Baker Eddy to support this conclusion.

Whatever the specific meaning which the apostle had in

thought when he wrote "I die daily" (I Cor. 15:31), it is surely evident from the context of his words that during his stormy but remarkably productive career he had faced death many times, and in so doing seems largely to have overcome the fear of it.

While many noted doctors and psychiatrists of our day have begun to record the effects of fear in contributing to mental and physical disorders of various kinds, more than eight decades ago Mrs. Eddy went even further, denouncing fear as the underlying cause of all sickness and constantly warning her students against it. Ample evidence to this effect can be found by reference to the complete concordances to her writings.

In its extreme form, fear has been known to be so acute as to result in death itself, and probably we have all heard of instances in which an individual's fear of taking an anaesthetic was so strong that when it was forcibly administered, he died as a result —not of the surgery involved, but of that fear. Christian Science banishes fear on the basis of an ever increasing recognition of the nature of God as the source and support of all His creation—as *Love,* in which fear cannot subsist, as the apostle John reminds us. May we not say that the progressive daily conquest of fear, through complete trust in the power of God, aids in counteracting in advance that climactic and ultimate type of fear which culminates in what is known as *death?*

Numerous references in St. Paul's epistles suggest that he was largely concerned with analyzing and answering for his readers the question of the nature of death, and with the daily overcoming of its various aspects. Moreover, he seems to have concluded that death is essentially mortal or material thinking, while by the same token, spiritual thinking is the basis of life and harmony: "For to be carnally minded is death; but to be spiritually minded is life and peace." (Rom. 8:6) Thus it would appear that the repeated stress laid by Christian Science on the persistent overcoming of material thinking and its replacement by the joyous spiritual consciousness of the presence and power of Life, God, contributes to the overcoming of death in our daily experience, thus providing a potent antidote which is available not merely at the instant of *death*—as that term is popularly used—but also in moments of grave danger.

Doubtless recalling Christ Jesus' designation of death as *sleep*, Mrs. Eddy writes of it in numerous passages in terms of illusion or delusion and describes it as a dream, indicating further her assurance that sooner or later man must awaken from the nightmare of death to the realization of its unreality and of the permanence and indestructibility of life, God-given and consequently God-sustained.

Christian Science maintains that healing can be accomplished at a distance just as readily as when the patient is in the presence of the Christian Science practitioner. I frankly admit that this was one of the things which puzzled me when I began the study of this Science, although for many years now I have repeatedly seen and experienced such healing.

In this connection it is important to remember that Christian Science treatment is never physical nor material; it is simply prayer, the joyous and certain recognition of the fact that God, the divine Mind, heals, or, more exactly, that there is in the final analysis nothing to be changed or healed excepting our thinking, since the creation of the one perfect God cannot be other than perfect, changeless, complete and whole.

Now since prayer, by its very nature and definition, has a spiritual basis, it follows that nearness cannot increase, nor can distance diminish, its efficacy. When thus viewed from the standpoint of prayer, what we often call *absent treatment* is freed from the element of scepticism sometimes associated with it in the thought of those to whom the phrase is unfamiliar.

The thought of prayer—or an uplifted spiritual consciousness—contributing to healing, not merely of those who are near, but also and equally of others who may be far distant when their need becomes known to the healer, was by no means invented by

Mary Baker Eddy, although she may be said to have rediscovered the effectiveness of this curative method.

Centuries before Jesus' time, Isaiah definitely associated this type of healing with God Himself, whom Christian Scientists unqualifiedly accept as the source and basis of all true healing. "Peace, peace to him that is far off, and to him that is near, saith the LORD; and I will heal him." (Isa. 57:19) Moreover it is evident from the pages of the Gospels that the Master himself could and did heal folk who were not in his immediate presence.

For example, a centurion's servant was cured in this manner (Luke 7), while the same was true of the son of a nobleman of Capernaum (John 4). The lad was "at the point of death," and his anxious father toiled some twenty miles up the steep hill road to Cana to enlist Jesus' aid, which was quickly given. Reassured by the Master's words "Go thy way; thy son liveth," he reached home the following day to find that the boy's fever had broken at the very time when his father talked with the good Physician, and that all was well. Here, then, is a further Biblical instance of what we term *absent treatment*.

"So far so good," someone may say, "but *that* was different! The one who wrought these cures was Christ Jesus himself, the founder of the Christian religion, and they occurred almost two thousand years ago in an obscure province in the Near East. Is there any accurate evidence to prove that such cures can still be effected in the twentieth century and in our own country?"

Yes, there is such evidence in abundance, and perhaps the clearest and fairest way to illustrate it is to record an experience of my own which came about many years ago. I wrote my parents in Scotland fully about it when it occurred and they kept the letter, which lies before me as I write, so in spite of the lapse of time the details are accurate.

As the opening sentence of my letter seems very much to the point, I quote it verbatim. "Vital though Christian Science is in my life, I have refrained from writing very much of the healings which the understanding of it has accomplished for me:—but since it has lately brought about my recovery from the effects of a very serious motor accident, I think it is only fair to you and to Christian Science that I should give you the facts of the case."

I was doing newspaper work in South Dakota at the time, which involved my calling upon many of the local farmers, and was several miles north of Clark, when the accident occurred. It was a dry, dusty summer afternoon and I was on my way home to my headquarters in Watertown, driving quite fast, when another car suddenly overtook and passed me going at an even higher rate of speed, and raising a thick cloud of dust. Before I could slow down appreciably, I dimly saw another car approaching directly ahead of me.

The road was fairly narrow, with deep ditches on either side, and a head-on collision seemed inevitable. In the fraction of a second before it occurred, I had time only to appeal almost involuntarily to my understanding of Christian Science, knowing that only one Mind, God, governed the situation, no matter how serious it might appear. Both cars automatically swerved in an effort to avoid a crash, but without success. As a result of the great force of the impact, the left front wheel came off the other car, and it turned off into the ditch, but providentially its six passengers remained unhurt.

After the crash, the brakes of my own car became locked and it went entirely out of control, slewing almost down into the ditch at the right and then back across the road. Experts who later examined the scene of the accident found evidence to show that my car turned over three times before coming to rest at the bottom of the left-hand ditch, facing in the opposite direction.

Finally, the door broke open and I was thrown out and pinned sideways across the hips between the running board and the ground, with the car resting upon me. The six people from the other car did their utmost to lift the car to free me, but without success. During this period of waiting I did not lose consciousness, although I had lost a considerable amount of blood, and I continued to claim and know the supporting and protecting power of God, as Christian Scientists make a practice of doing, especially in any emergency. Then, too, I felt deeply grateful for the fact that I was still alive and, above all, that the others were unhurt.

In a few minutes (although it seemed much longer to me) a passing motorist from Watertown stopped and by using a jack was able to raise the car sufficiently so that they could pull me out. I could neither walk nor stand at this point. Broken glass was scattered in every direction and minute fragments of it were lying on my face almost in my eyes, but one of the bystanders was able to remove them before they did any harm. There was a cut on my chin, and my head was bruised, as were other parts of my body. I had deep gashes on both hands.

They rushed me to Clark, the nearest town, insisting that I receive first aid to the extent of putting stitches in my hands. The surgeon warned me to expect sharp pain when he used his needle, but actually, to his surprise, I felt scarcely any pain, although he broke a needle during the operation. He and the men who carried me into his office seemed much more concerned over the situation than I was, so I told them Scotch stories to ease the tension.

(It is only fair to add that there are many instances in which surgery has been carried out solely on the basis of prayer as practiced by Christian Scientists. For example, some years later, during an Atlantic crossing, I received a very severe blow on one of my fingers. A medical nurse of my acquaintance insisted on examining it, and assured me that a bone was broken and that I must visit the ship's doctor. Instead of doing so I applied to the situation my growing understanding of Christian Science, with its assurance of the unbroken perfection of man, and in a day or two was using my typewriter as actively as ever.)

While lying on the stretcher in the surgeon's office in Clark,

I telephoned a Christian Scientist in Watertown, but as I could not at this stage hold the phone myself, the surgeon's assistant held it for me. At my request, my friend telegraphed a Christian Science practitioner in New York—some 1,500 miles distant—asking for absent treatment, which was promptly commenced. Although Christian Science practitioners are available in South Dakota, and indeed all over the country, I selected this one in New York, not of necessity, but because I knew her well, and she had done quick and effective work for me on other occasions.

I expressed deep appreciation to the surgeon for his concern and kindly help, but explained to him that, as a Christian Scientist, I wished to be taken home rather than to a hospital. Arrangements for this were quickly made, and the man who had driven me to Clark from the scene of the accident drove me home to Watertown. He admitted afterwards that he did so with considerable misgivings, judging from the way I then looked that I "might die on his hands" before he covered the thirty or so miles to the city.

My friends awaited my arrival and I was carefully carried in and put to bed in my own room. From that night on, two of them—also students of Christian Science—nursed me night and day for almost two weeks, and I am most grateful for all they and others did for me at that time.

A required X-ray examination showed that while no bones were broken, the sacroiliac joint and the tip of the spine were displaced, in addition to the bruising and straining of the hip muscles.

The report about the wrecked car was more discouraging than that about the driver! The side of the car next the driving seat was almost severed from the rest of the body. All four fenders were crushed and bent. At least one door was off. The wheels were buckled and out of alignment, and three of them had to be replaced. The windshield was smashed and the radiator severely damaged.

Several of those who examined the car, later expressed to me great surprise that I escaped alive and without permanent injury. A business man in Clark, whom I met after returning to work, said he had often thought about that accident and "didn't know how in the world" any of those involved survived it. Another man told me that in his opinion "it was a miracle."

Judging from what I afterwards learned from other clients in the vicinity of Clark, at least 75 per cent of them had heard it definitely stated that I was both dead and buried. Consequently many of them were both amazed and startled to see me when I next visited them, which made me feel rather like a modern Lazarus!

For some time after the accident, we kept in almost daily touch by telegraph with my Christian Science practitioner in New York, who did excellent work on each phase of the case, while I myself continued my customary daily study of the Bible and the Christian Science textbook. At no time was I tempted to use any medication. Improvement was steady from the first day. Not only were the more obvious physical effects of the accident progressively healed, but a feeling of great weakness, due apparently to loss of blood, was also overcome quickly and effectively.

I have before me an exact record of the progress of the healing, and feel that it will be of interest to the reader if I cite it briefly here. The accident occurred on Wednesday, August 14th, at about five in the afternoon. By Saturday the cut on my chin had healed perfectly, leaving no scar; I could sit up in bed, and my appetite was excellent. On Monday, the 19th, I sat up in a chair in my room for about two hours. The following Monday, August 26th, I stood alone for the first time since the accident, and was able to sit up in a chair a good part of the day. Between the 26th and 30th, I began gradually to walk a few steps, and the following day got downstairs with the aid of two walking sticks. Tuesday, September 3rd, I bought a new car and drove it a short distance. About the middle of that week I found I no longer needed the canes. By this time the cuts on my hands had healed perfectly. Monday, September 9th (26 days after the accident), I returned to work fully recovered.

In Christian Science practice, it often happens that a wonderful healing comes about so naturally and steadily that one fails to realize how much has been overcome. The accident which I have described was undoubtedly a most serious one, as can be seen from the details I have given and the opinions I have quoted regarding it; and I am convinced that nothing but the power of God could have brought me back to health and strength in so short a time. Not only so, but I feel that without the realization of that power, by myself and by the Christian Science practitioner who helped me, I might well not have survived to relate the experience.

This episode, which occurred while I was still quite a young student of Christian Science—about two years after I joined a branch church of our denomination—made me renewedly grateful for a growing realization of the healing and protecting power of God, which can be gained through the study and practice of Christian Science. This was yet another proof to me (and there had been many before and have been many more since) that God can and does heal men now, as surely and effectively as He healed them in Jesus' day. Moreover, it was to me a particularly clear example of the effectiveness of the *absent treatment* practiced by Christian Scientists.

As I looked back on the experience at the time, and have done so since, it has taught me many other things. One of these is the deep value and potency of knowing and affirming the ever-operative government of the one perfect Mind, which is God, as I did in that instant before the accident occurred. I am convinced that this heartfelt declaration—this momentary prayer—contributed directly to the protection which was manifested throughout the experience that followed.

In spite of the collision and the wreck of the car, the fact remains that the six others involved in the accident were unhurt, while even my own injuries were relatively minor in comparison with what might perhaps have been expected to occur as the result of a car falling on me and showering me with broken glass —if, indeed, I survived at all. Within a few weeks, as I have explained, I returned to work.

In short, it seems to me a particularly outstanding proof not only of the healing power made available through Christian Science, but also of the protection which can come to those who earnestly seek to make both the teachings and the practice of the Master Christian their daily guide, as Mrs. Eddy taught her followers to do.

Recognizing the apparent power of suggestion, any Christian Scientist is well aware that the recounting of such an occurrence in vivid detail must be vigorously offset by the realization on his own part, and that of the reader or listener, of the ultimate unreality and powerlessness of such conditions, which do not exist in God's kingdom of perfect harmony. Man, the child of God, is not governed by chance or accident. "Under divine Providence," Mrs. Eddy reminds us, "there can be no accidents, since there is no room for imperfection in perfection." (*Science and Health:* p. 424)

We maintain that to God, who made all things good, accidents, cancers, epidemics and the like, are devoid of reality. My realization of this at the time of the "accident" helped to nullify its insistent claims upon my attention, and contributed to my healing.

It may be added that Christian Scientists do not blandly ignore accident, disease, sin or error in any form. They realize that to the person facing such problems they are far from imaginary, and may even constitute settled convictions; thus it is with compassionate understanding that the practitioner helps his patients to see that these are false arguments and that, as such, they have no place in God's universe, despite their insistent claims to reality. He explains that because God never made, nor does He maintain, such fears or difficulties, they are groundless, devoid of authority or power and cannot continue to hold man in bondage.

A Christian Scientist is a humanitarian, ever eager to help and encourage those still groping for a deeper understanding of the true nature of God and man, which is the basis of Christian Science healing.

NINE

MISSIONARIES OF
THE CHRISTIAN SCIENCE CHURCH

AMONG Christian churches, missionary activity is considered of vital importance, and the Christian Science church is no exception. In fact we maintain that, in accordance with Christ Jesus' express demand, it is our privilege and obligation to go "into all the world," not only spreading the good news of Christianity, but also healing the sick.

As a theological student in Edinburgh, I was active in Presbyterian home mission work and was also deeply interested in foreign missions. Attendance as a delegate at a World Missionary Congress held in Glasgow further increased my interest, and at one time I seriously considered going to India myself as a missionary. While my plans did not develop in that direction, and I eventually came to the United States, my eager desire to spread the Gospel has continued, and has been in no degree lessened, but rather increased, by my study and practice of Christian Science. This great subject, with its essentially practical interpretation of Christianity, means so much to me that I am eager to share my understanding of it in any way that I can.

It is true that the Christian Science Church does not appoint official resident missionaries at home or abroad, as do other denominations; but in so far as each one of its far-flung members is in effect an unofficial emissary of our faith and of its Discoverer

134

and Founder, Mary Baker Eddy, people throughout the world have an opportunity of seeing and hearing what Christian Science is, and what it can accomplish. This does not mean that we seek to enforce our way of thinking upon others, but we do try to be ever ready to provide the "cup of cold water" of the Master's illustration. It is for others to choose whether or not they will accept it.

A *missionary*, as the derivation of the term indicates, is "one sent forth" to spread an idea, and more especially the Gospel; and while, in the case of Christian Scientists, the motive power is an inner urge, it is none the less compelling. Our deep gratitude for what Christian Science has done for us, and our assurance of what it can do for the world, makes the sincere student of this subject both eager and alert to do his part in sharing its message.

St. Paul speaks of himself and his converts as "ambassadors for Christ"—personal representatives of the Master. It is in the same spirit that active members of our denomination do their utmost, whether in public or in private life, to prove worthy of the challenging and responsible task of representing Christ Jesus and that essentially demonstrable interpretation of his teachings known as Christian Science.

My experience has been that in many cases—including my own —the evident results of its healing, supporting and harmonizing influence have done far more than words to introduce it to those searching for a more practical form of religion.

In short, each member of our church is a missionary for it, and can further its spread by both living and proving his understanding of its teachings, while being prepared at the proper time either to speak of the nature of these teachings or to refer the inquirer to the sources from which he can obtain for himself detailed and authentic information.

It need hardly be stated that first among these is the Christian Science textbook, *Science and Health with Key to the Scriptures,* in which Mary Baker Eddy sets forth what she justly considered to be the full and complete statement of the teachings and practice of Christian Science. This book is available in most public libraries, and can of course be obtained or studied in every Christian Science Reading Room.

The challenging and exacting task of accurately translating the precisely phrased and deeply spiritual statements of *Science and Health* into other languages has been successfully accomplished. It is now obtainable in Dutch, French, German, Spanish or Swedish, with the original English text facing each page of translation, while it is also available in Braille and on "talking book" records.

In further performing our role as missionaries of our church it is customary for us to introduce the inquirer to our regular Sunday services and to our Wednesday meetings, both of which are described in an earlier chapter. The section of the Wednesday meeting devoted to the giving of personal experiences and testimonies witnessing to the practical efficacy of Christian Science in the healing and prevention of sickness and the solution of problems of all kinds—and, above all, in providing a deeper understanding of God—contributes directly to the missionary activity of our denomination. While many visitors to such meetings eventually become active students and church members themselves, all are most welcome to attend and no pressure is put upon them to affiliate themselves with Christian Science.

A further significant and distinctive aspect of the work of promoting the spread of Christian Science is found in the publication and distribution of the various Christian Science periodicals which we sometimes term "our silent missionaries." These periodicals were established by Mrs. Eddy herself at various times to meet the growing needs of the movement she founded.

Within eight years of the publication of the first edition of *Science and Health,* its author announced the compelling need for a newspaper both published and edited by Christian Scientists. It was typical of Mrs. Eddy that she lost no time in putting this idea into practical effect, for in April of 1883 appeared the first issue of the *Journal of Christian Science,* later named *The Christian Science Journal.* In its early days it appeared every second month, as a small pamphlet of eight pages, containing advertising, some news of the day and articles for the home, in addition, of course, to articles on Christian Science and its practical application to the meeting of human needs. Modest as was its beginning, it marked the commencement of a series of publications which through the years have done much to introduce Christian Science to the reading public. Mrs. Eddy herself was the first editor and publisher of the *Journal,* which soon outgrew its original limited format to become a regular monthly magazine, including today some fifty or more pages in addition to a complete directory of recognized Christian Science Churches and Reading Rooms, besides Teachers, Practitioners and qualified Nurses—throughout the world. Christian Science Societies and College Organizations are also listed.

As the *Journal* developed, and other periodicals were founded to supplement it, news items and secular advertising were omitted. In its present form it includes editorials, together with other articles on various aspects of Christian Science, contributed by members of The Mother Church. A considerable section is always devoted to carefully verified testimonies confirming the healing power of Christian Science, submitted by grateful students from this and other lands. Now in its seventy-sixth year, the *Journal* is still the official organ of The First Church of Christ, Scientist, in Boston, Massachusetts.

For fifteen years the *Journal* remained our only regular periodical, but in 1898 Mrs. Eddy established *The Christian Science Weekly,* while a few months later she gave it its present name of the *Christian Science Sentinel.* This publication enabled her to keep in more direct contact with her rapidly expanding church than was possible through the medium of a monthly.

Originally printed on pages of roughly quarto size, it has appeared since 1942 in the familiar "digest" format. Like the *Journal,* the *Sentinel* contains chiefly articles and editorials on

Christian Science, testimonies of healing, and occasional reports on the varied activities of our organization. It also prints announcements of Christian Science lectures and transcripts of weekly radio programs sponsored by our denomination and entitled "How Christian Science Heals." Both these aspects of our work will be discussed later.

As the Christian Science movement continued to spread and became widely known in other lands, its Founder inaugurated the policy of making it possible for those unacquainted or but slightly acquainted with English, to read about Christian Science in their own languages. One of the first steps in this direction came in 1903, when Mrs. Eddy authorized the publication of *Der Herold der Christian Science* in German. Somewhat similar in content to *The Christian Science Journal,* although not directly corresponding to it, *Der Herold* appears monthly. In making this new departure, Mrs. Eddy was enabled to spread even more widely the good news of Truth's universal activity and practical availability.

Following the lead of this precedent, a French *Herald* appeared in due course—in 1917—at the time of the First World War. This, too, is a monthly, as is the Braille (English) Edition which began in 1931. Quarterly editions of *The Herald of Christian Science* appear at present in Dutch, Danish, Norwegian, Swedish, Italian, Portuguese, and Spanish, while pamphlets are available in some fourteen different languages.

All these publications are printed with the English text and foreign translation on opposite pages. This device has been found to be most helpful by students who are learning English, particularly because of the uniformly scholarly quality of the translation.

By far the most ambitious of the various periodicals inaugurated by Mary Baker Eddy, and one of the most widely known, is *The Christian Science Monitor.* In 1908, towards the close of her long and active career, she became convinced that the denomination she founded should have a daily newspaper, which is now observing its fiftieth year of continuous and successful publication. It will be recalled that when establishing *The Christian Science Journal,* a quarter of a century earlier, she had thought of it in terms of a newspaper, but the *Monitor* appearing daily (except Sundays and national holidays) is a newspaper in the most generally accepted sense.

Mrs. Eddy's remarkable vision and courage are no more clearly manifested than in the founding of *The Christian Science Monitor.* To plan for and bring into being a daily paper and, moreover, an international one, was a project to tax the ingenuity and resources of the most active and experienced journalist or executive. When we consider that Mrs. Eddy was at the time only a few years short of ninety, her initiative and achievement in founding the *Monitor* are seen as the more remarkable.

Apparently she had been giving serious consideration to this project for some time, but it was not until July of 1908 that she notified The Christian Science Board of Directors of her plan; while on the 8th of the following month she wrote to those who would be most directly concerned with putting it into effect, the Trustees of The Christian Science Publishing Society, announcing to them the fact that in her judgment it was essential for the development of the Cause she founded, and headed, that a daily newspaper be started without delay. Moreover she stipulated that it should be named *The Christian Science Monitor.* (See Wilbur: *Life of Mary Baker Eddy:* p. 359)

Since the first issue of the *Monitor* actually appeared on November 25th of the same year, there remained only three and a half months in which to plan, develop and complete what might justly be viewed as a monumental enterprise. The plant already in use for printing *The Christian Science Journal,* together with the *Sentinel* and *Herald,* had to be expanded and new buildings erected. Suitable printing presses had to be planned, ordered and installed; editors, reporters and technical workers of various kinds had to be found and employed—to mention only a small part of the many arrangements which must be made and made quickly.

Bearing all this in mind, it says much for the vision of the Directors and the Trustees and evidences their trust in Mrs. Eddy's judgment and timing, as well as their loyalty to her, that they accepted with alacrity what may well have seemed an almost unsurmountable responsibility, and proceeded to take all the necessary steps to establish this newspaper as a journalistic reality. Christian Scientists throughout the field were prompt to do their part in shouldering the expense of the new venture, contributing in a remarkably short space of time almost four hundred thousand dollars to aid in meeting the initial outlay.

True, there were some who questioned the wisdom of the title which Mrs. Eddy had selected for her paper—*The Christian Science Monitor*. Bearing in mind the generally accepted fact that even weekly denominational journals are seldom financially successful, and that presumably a denominational daily, if one had the temerity to appear, would be even less likely to succeed, they sought to convince Mrs. Eddy of the advisability of choosing some less provocative title. However, she stood firmly by her original decision, and her courage and foresight in doing so have been amply justified with the passage of time.

Throughout the first fifty years of its continuous publication, *The Christian Science Monitor* has come to be regarded as virtually a synonym for clean, courageous and outstanding journalism. Its subscription list is by no means limited to members of our denomination. It is widely read, and as widely respected, by people of all faiths and in all walks of life who are interested in accurate, constructive reporting, and in a newspaper which they can welcome into their homes, and allow their children to read freely, assured that they will not be misled by the sensationalism and destructive reading matter all too often appearing in many daily papers even though they may be otherwise acceptable.

Through the years I have often written for the *Monitor* myself

—feature articles on the Bible and on archaeology, book reviews, occasional news stories and brief articles on Christian Science— and when acquaintances who are not Christian Scientists have asked where my articles appeared, they have uniformly spoken in complimentary terms of the high standards and fine reputation of *The Christian Science Monitor,* and many have proved to be personally familiar with it.

Under the caption "SOMETHING IN A NAME," the leading editorial which appeared in the first issue of the *Monitor* records in Mary Baker Eddy's own ringing words her policy for the paper she founded, together with the purpose of each of the other periodicals which she had already successfully established.

"I have given the name to all the Christian Science periodicals. The first was *The Christian Science Journal,* designed to put on record the divine Science of Truth; the second I entitled *Sentinel,* intended to hold guard over Truth, Life, and Love; the third, *Der Herold der Christian Science,* to proclaim the universal activity and availability of Truth; the next I named *Monitor,* to spread undivided the Science that operates unspent. The object of the *Monitor* is to injure no man, but to bless all mankind." (See *Miscellany:* p. 353)

The high purpose proclaimed in that concluding sentence set the keynote for the *Monitor's* success, and its editors through the years have consistently upheld this standard, never overlooking the healing power of truth, even when reporting the news of the day.

It may be added that the *Monitor* and members of its staff, have been recipients of numerous awards, attesting the uniformly high caliber of its journalism and the sustained respect it has enjoyed since its inception.

It is sometimes asked how *The Christian Science Monitor* can fulfill its claim to be "An International Daily Newspaper" when it is published exclusively in Boston, Massachusetts. For one thing, it was Mrs. Eddy's specific request that the members of the denomination she founded should subscribe to the *Monitor.*

As thousands of our members live in many parts of the world, the fact that copies go out regularly to subscribers in the United States and some 120 other countries automatically demands, and contributes to, the international character of the paper's coverage.

Like other metropolitan "dailies," the *Monitor* has its own staff of trained correspondents and reporters in all quarters of the globe; but, bearing in mind its unique position as a daily paper read all over the world, its editors see to it that substantial attention is given to news and events in many countries.

This provides an additional reason why *The Christian Science Monitor* is so widely used in schools. Not only does it refrain from stressing the morbid and destructive "news" and headlines all too often evident in many other papers, but also it provides up-to-date and interesting news, information and pictures concerning foreign lands—invaluable in the classroom.

Throughout its columns there is a consistent effort to view the news of the day in its broadest significance, placing it in the framework of history, and to handle constructively any problem or catastrophe demanding attention because of its news interest. The contribution to world peace and international understanding afforded by such a wide policy will be obvious to the discerning reader.

As an article in *Time Magazine* (January 27, 1958: p. 42) points out, the *Monitor* is "firmly fixed as one of the world's most respected dailies" and "gets the ultimate tribute of the news profession: its subscribers include 4,000 editors and newspapers throughout the world, some of whom pay as much as $1,000 a year to have their copies air-mailed (worldwide, first-class-mail subscription rate: $18)."

Because of the expense necessarily involved in receiving the special air-mail edition of the *Monitor* in distant lands, the great majority of subscribers abroad still receive it by surface-mail. Consequently it may take many days, or even weeks, to reach its destination. How, the reader may ask, does a daily paper fare under such conditions?

In the case of the *Monitor* this unavoidable delay is not so serious as one might suppose. Realizing that ordinarily it can be read on the day of publication only by those within easy reach of Boston, its editors prepare an edition primarily for local readers, while its other editions, and especially the papers which go overseas, are so designed as to be up to date not only when printed, but also for a long time to come. This helps to explain why the *Monitor,* while appearing six days a week, is often referred to as one of the Christian Science *periodicals.*

It is not easy even to outline the contents of a typical issue of the *Monitor* since it contains such a wide variety of interesting and helpful information. Besides national and international news stories, book reviews and penetrating editorials, it has its financial and sports pages, and is noted for its feature articles and special series on subjects of current interest. It has its women's page, and pages specially designed for young people, while discussions of books and the theatre, and informative articles on scientific developments, music, the garden, and many other topics, serve the varied interests of its readers in many lands.

One of the *Monitor's* best known features is its Home Forum page, generally devoted to essays and excerpts from good literature with, as a rule, an illustration of a painting or famous sculpture, etc., with historical and descriptive notes. This is the one page including a brief, simply-worded daily article on Christian Science, usually accompanied by a translation into some language other than English—again providing a reminder of the fact that the *Monitor* travels far afield.

It is a journalistic axiom that no daily newspaper can exist without advertising, and Mary Baker Eddy, an alert business woman as well as a religious leader, stipulated that the paper she founded should carry advertising from its first issue. One characteristic of *Monitor* advertising is its wide scope. It is the rule rather than the exception for me to see in the edition which reaches me in Greenwich, Connecticut, advertisements from many parts of the world, including, for example, England,

Switzerland, Germany, Australia, South Africa—and from all parts of the United States and Canada. This does not imply that the advertising is purely national or international, for many of the merchants in our own town advertise regularly in the *Monitor.*

Another aspect of *Monitor* advertising which appeals particularly to the advertiser is the practical and vocal response of *Monitor* readers, who make it a point, where possible, to patronize those who have seen fit to support their newspaper by advertising in it and to let them know that both their products and their advertising are appreciated. Recently when making some purchases in a local store I thanked the proprietor for his advertising in the *Monitor.* He was not a Christian Scientist, but assured me that no one would have to convince him of the value of using this advertising medium for each advertisement quickly paid for itself by providing direct and practical results. It may be added that the *Monitor* accepts none of the lucrative advertising promoting drugs, tobacco or liquor. As the use of these in any form is not consonant with the teachings of Christian Science, it is obvious that the promotion of their use would likewise be banned.

In addition to the circulation of the *Monitor* and the other Christian Science periodicals by the usual methods of annual subscription and the sale of individual copies, they are also widely circulated in other ways. For example, our churches have active Literature Distribution Committees, which make free copies available in many public places—railroad stations, waiting rooms and so forth. Many people have made their first contact with Christian Science in this way.

In some of the larger port cities, such as New York and London, a Harbor Committee distributes to ships thousands of pieces of our denominational literature and many encouraging reports of the interest aroused and help received, show the value of this branch of our church's missionary activity among seamen.

Whether or not the receipt of such free copies of literature ever results in any direct affiliation with Christian Science, the helpful and constructive reading matter which they provide is part of our contribution to progress and enlightenment, and to public health, for in many instances healing has resulted from the careful reading of these periodicals and the acceptance of their practical messages of hope and harmony.

The Christian Science Publishing Society naturally concentrates upon the written word in spreading the gospel of Christian Science, but Mary Baker Eddy saw the wisdom of using still other methods in introducing to the public at large the faith she founded.

As early as 1898, she established *The Christian Science Board of Lectureship,* consisting of cultured and experienced men and women, qualified both intellectually and spiritually to address large audiences on the subject of Christian Science. Appointments, and in most cases re-appointments, to this Board are made annually by the governing body of our church, The Christian Science Board of Directors, in Boston.

Prior to 1898, Mrs. Eddy herself had given many successful lectures on the subject so close to her heart, and in inaugurating the Board of Lectureship she made it possible for the work to be carried farther afield, until now such lectures can be heard in all parts of the English-speaking world. Besides their constant activities in this country and in Europe, our lecturers travel to South America and the West Indies, to Egypt and South Africa, to Australia and New Zealand, to India, China, Japan, and many other distant points. Such lectures are also given in other languages from time to time, such as French and German, in order to make the good news of the practicality of Christian Science as widely available as possible.

The content of a Christian Science lecture is largely left to the discretion of the individual speaker, with the proviso that the text of each lecture is subject to the approval of The Christian

Science Board of Directors before its delivery. While, then, they are not given extemporaneously, in the strict sense of the term, this is found in practice to enhance their value, since their substance and wording have been carefully considered in advance. Also, their message is sufficiently inspiring to all concerned to bear repetition.

One of the main objects of such lectures is to present to the public in simple and readily understandable form a brief outline of what Christian Science is and what it does. Obviously any one lecture can give only a glimpse of such a wide subject, but each is interesting and provocative on its own, and provides an introduction to the whole. Our lecturers are also expected, when necessary, to correct courteously and calmly for the information of the audience any current misapprehension regarding Christian Science. Then, too, each lecturer explains something of the essentially Biblical authority for this Science, besides bearing witness to the facts concerning the life and work of its Discoverer and Founder, Mary Baker Eddy.

Even from this brief outline of the content of our Christian Science lectures, the reader will see that they are primarily intended for the information of the public, although many members of our own denomination attend and profit by them. Thus they correspond somewhat in their approach to the direct missionary activity carried on by other churches, although varying from it in that our lecturers travel constantly from place to place, and often from country to country.

Because of their plan of reaching the general public, Christian Science lectures are always given without charge and all are welcome to attend. Often they are held in the edifice of the Christian Science church (or society) sponsoring the lecture, and sometimes in a public auditorium, but in any event the lecturer's fee and any expenses connected with the giving of the lecture are paid by the local church. As those who attend are considered our guests, every effort is made to provide for their convenience and comfort. Special seats are usually reserved for those attending one of our lectures for the first time, and for those who because of age or physical disability require special attention.

The Mother Church in Boston and each of its branches throughout the world sponsors at least one lecture annually, and in most cases several are given, with the result that the activities of The Christian Science Board of Lectureship are truly world-wide.

Many Christian Science lectures are broadcast by major radio stations at the time they are given, indicating our readiness to use modern methods of communication in presenting to an increasingly wide audience the facts regarding Christian Science and its message of comfort, hope, healing and salvation to all mankind.

One of the most interesting developments along this line within recent years has come with the inauguration of a series of programs entitled "How Christian Science Heals." Sponsored and produced by The Mother Church in Boston, these programs, generally about fifteen minutes in length, are transcribed and are at present broadcast over approximately 800 radio stations throughout the world.

Each program presents a personal but dignified account of healing, protection or enlightenment, given by the individual who experienced it through the study and application of Christian Science. Healings recently recounted on such programs include the cure of tuberculosis, cancer, broken bones, influenza, alcoholism, severe burns, children's diseases—and indeed of all kinds of infirmities. Often the cure has been acknowledged by the same physician who had previously given up the case as incurable.

These brief, but obviously sincere testimonies are followed by a short explanation and expansion—by the moderator of the program—of the facts presented, with reference to the Bible and the Christian Science textbook; and they conclude with a solo, generally a selection from our Hymnal. As already mentioned, transcripts appear weekly in the *Christian Science Sentinel*.

This type of missionary activity is proving remarkably successful in presenting to the radio audiences of many lands the fact of healing through the understanding of God, as taught by Christian Science, and many thousands of requests for literature and further information on this vital subject are received annually.

In many parts of the United States, our churches arrange for the regular or periodical broadcasting of their Sunday services, while upon occasion the Christian Science church takes its turn with other denominations in presenting special programs sponsored by leading radio networks, with a view to encouraging public and individual worship, as well as acquainting their audiences with the teachings of various churches. It may be added that the stimulating news broadcasts conducted by the editor of *The Christian Science Monitor* have enjoyed a wide listening audience over many years.

With the advent and wide expansion of television, our church has also entered that field. The "Television Edition" of "How Christian Science Heals" of course makes even more vivid the experiences presented, since the viewer can both hear and see the individual telling of his own healing. These programs are now carried by approximately 150 stations.

The important work accomplished by *Christian Science Reading Rooms* throughout the world may justifiably be included in this outline of the missionary activities of our church.

Each of our churches has its Reading Room, frequently located in a separate building, and in many instances in the business sections of large cities, within reach of a wide segment of the busy public. These Reading Rooms form an integral part of the Christian Science organization, and are available for the free use of all who wish to avail themselves of the opportunity which they afford for quiet study and spiritual refreshment.

At every Christian Science Reading Room one can read, borrow, or purchase the Bible, as well as all authorized Christian

Science literature, including *Science and Health* and the other writings by Mary Baker Eddy. The librarian is always happy to answer questions, or to refer the visitor to books or articles which may provide his answer.

For the Christian Scientist, these Reading Rooms provide quiet oases for study in any town, no matter how many thousands of miles from home; while many who are not members, or even attendants of our church, regularly visit and enjoy them.

The reader may recall that when I decided not to continue my preparation for the ministry of the Presbyterian Church, on seriously taking up the study of Christian Science, I forfeited the permission granted to me, as a British citizen, to study in the United States, and moved to Canada. Arriving in Ottawa, where I was a complete stranger, my first step was to seek out the Christian Science Reading Room in that city. The opportunity it afforded for quiet study of Christian Science, and the friendly helpfulness of the librarian, meant a great deal to me at this somewhat lonely period in my experience.

I feel that my regular visits to that Reading Room contributed directly to the various unfoldments which quickly came about, including not only the finding of a satisfactory place to live, but also of employment which met my financial needs, while broadening my experience. My personal gratitude for the vision and thoughtfulness of Mrs. Eddy in establishing such free public Reading Rooms for the benefit of all who wish to profit by them, has increased through the years.

It may be of interest to record here that Christian Science Reading Rooms have readily available bound volumes of the monthly *Christian Science Journal* and weekly *Christian Science Sentinel* extending back, in many cases, to the time of their original publication prior to 1900.

Because of the fully authenticated testimonies of healing, and well-written articles on Christian Science contained in these volumes, they are both timeless and timely, as well as practical, and they are still widely read by visitors to our Reading Rooms.

It goes without saying that Mary Baker Eddy's own writings, dating from 1875 on, are perhaps even more eagerly read than they were at the time of their first appearance, and the various biographies of Mrs. Eddy, and books tracing the history of our church, are found invaluable by the sincere student.

By way of contrast, my experience with many religious periodicals and religious books of other types, has been that they rarely, if ever, maintain such an active status, even after a relatively short time.

From what has been recorded in this chapter, I believe it will be clear to the reader that the missionary work of our denomination, while differing in some respects from that of other churches, is none the less active, and there are many indications showing its effectiveness in introducing to the public this essentially practical and provable Science of Christianity.

Every human being desires and should have, health and happiness, harmony and security, progress and prosperity, and the fact that Christian Science shows how such rich benefits can be obtained, on the basis of the consistent practice of effective prayer, and the progressive recognition and acceptance of man's spiritual relationship to God, as taught in the Scriptures, provides a beacon of hope to many searching for a clearer understanding of God, and of man's heritage as a son of God.

TEN

THE EDUCATIONAL SYSTEM OF CHRISTIAN SCIENCE

"**E**DUCATION is the mother of wisdom and prudence." So runs a free translation of the Greek motto of the Edinburgh Academy which I attended as a boy and which was almost within a stone's throw of a Christian Science church, although I knew nothing of Christian Science at that time. The value of education goes without saying, and it may be assumed that every denomination stresses the religious training of its members and especially, perhaps, of their children, and it is with a view to outlining the distinctive approach of the Christian Science church to education that this chapter is included. Bearing in mind the scope of this Science, and the fact that it is applicable to every aspect of human experience, it may be noted at the outset that the training it provides is correspondingly broad. As Mrs. Eddy herself expressed it in an article regarding the college she founded: "This Christian educational system is established on a broad and liberal basis. Law and order characterize its work and secure a thorough preparation of the student for practice." (*Miscellany:* p. 245)

Since Christian Science was a discovery—and one which, moreover, was made somewhat less than a century ago—it is obvious

151

that its Founder must explain and teach to others this new-old way of life, if it were to expand in even the least degree. It is a historical, and in many ways a phenomenal fact that Christian Science has indeed expanded in the past nine decades as a result of the inspired leadership of this quiet refined New England woman, Mary Baker Eddy, until now it numbers many thousands of members and is known and practiced in every quarter of the globe. Thus we may well inquire as to what methods of teaching she herself employed and what system she established to ensure the extension and perpetuation of the faith she founded, and the continued correctness and clarity of the teachings and practices which gave it its original vitality and contribute to its growing success.

Having once received her own healing on the basis of prayer and as a result of consecrated study of the Bible, she turned her attention almost exclusively to the Scriptures for several years. Grateful as she was for the healing she had experienced, she realized that through it she had made a discovery which could be of untold value to the human race, and she would not rest until she understood, at least in a measure, how and why her recovery had come about, so that this rich treasure of healing and enlightenment could be shared with those prepared to accept it. It was as if she stood on the threshold of a new and uncharted universe, a universe of ideas, where time and space would no longer serve as guide or gauge, and where each one must learn for himself to weigh and grapple with intangible forces, hitherto unknown to him. The challenge of grasping and interpreting such ideas, and of introducing this mental discipline to others, now claimed the full attention of the Discoverer of Christian Science.

As a young woman, she had had some experience in teaching. Besides conducting a Sunday School class in connection with the Congregational Church of which she was then a member, she taught upon occasion in the New Hampshire Conference Seminary, and established one of the first nursery schools in her native state. However, these activities provided little direct preparation for the teaching of Christian Science. In this work she had to be guided and was invariably guided, by inspiration. Feeling that the God whom she identified as Mind had revealed this Science through her, she was assured that He would supply increasing understanding of it, together with the ability to impart it successfully to others.

Although she had seen and felt the efficacy of spiritual healing in her own experience even from her childhood, and although she recognized the untold possibilities inherent in Christian Science as she had discovered it, she was ever conscious of the necessity of finding a clear and thorough method of communicating it to others, so that its undeniable benefit for mankind should never again slip into oblivion.

It was through years of patient and ceaseless work, therefore, that she prepared herself for the task of readily, easily and accurately detecting, and of speedily correcting, any uncertainty or vagueness of understanding in the thought of those who would come to learn from her about metaphysical Science. Having discussed her ideas with any who would listen, as well as having tested her method in every practical way through healing, she was now ready to teach others, without fear or doubt concerning the future stability and unfoldment of her great subject.

Her first student was Hiram Crafts, a shoe worker in Lynn, Massachusetts, where Mrs. Eddy (then Mrs. Patterson) lived at this period. From this small and simple beginning (reminiscent of the Master's contacts with humble fisherfolk), her teaching work developed. With Crafts, and gradually with others, she shared her notes and manuscripts which, combined with her personal instruction and, of course, with deep study of the Bible, gave these early followers their first contact with Christian Science.

Her work with Hiram Crafts and other individual students or inquirers, continued for several years, but as early as 1870 (five years before *Science and Health* was published) we find her conducting for the first time a class on the subject of Christian Science. It is surely significant that Samuel P. Bancroft, one of the members of this first class, later recalled that "at all times she seemed conscious of a wisdom beyond her own." (See Judge Clifford P. Smith: *Historical Sketches:* p. 133.)

As interest in her teaching and healing work grew and adherents to the system of Christian Science increased in number, it became imperative that her individual teaching should be supplemented by the work of others, if this new movement were to develop. This would also leave her more free for carrying on the unprecedented and extremely demanding work of writing, organization and leadership for which, as events proved, she was peculiarly fitted.

The plan which Mrs. Eddy worked out to meet this need will be examined shortly, but at this point we may look for a moment at the method she used in instructing her students as reflected in the recollections of some of those who studied with her in her latest classes conducted about the turn of the century. From that time on until her passing in 1910 her activities, while vigorous as ever, lay along other lines.

I have had the privilege of talking with a number of those who attended her classes in the 80's and 90's, and from what they had to say and from reminiscences which have appeared in print from time to time, I hope I can convey something of the impression made upon her pupils, not only by her message, but also by the way in which she impressed it upon her audience.

The constant activity and alertness of her thought, and her equally constant preoccupation with the spiritually mental aspects of existence, made her appear much younger than her years. For example, when she was but a few years short of seventy, her students were impressed by her vigor, beauty and youthful appearance, and similar statements come from those who knew her at other periods. All agree that her eyes were particularly striking. Because of their depth and almost luminous radiance it was often difficult to determine their color, but they are generally conceded to have been a deep blue, so dark that at times they almost seemed to be black. Large, clear and unwavering, they possessed a penetrating quality which appeared to probe deeply into her students' thoughts, but with invariable kindliness and understanding. Above all, they expressed intelligence and constant awareness.

Rarely, if ever, did anything escape Mrs. Eddy's notice, especially when she was conducting a class. She gave of herself and of her understanding without stint, and expected of her students close and undivided attention. Assured of her ability to impart her subject, she seems to have been equally confident that her students could readily retain, or could at least school themselves to retain, the spiritually rich lessons which she provided for them. It was no doubt for this reason, among others, that notetaking was not allowed without her express permission, and if any surreptitious jottings were put down, she would pause in her instruction to give an imperative reminder that notebooks were not to be used.

In most of her classes the question and answer method of teaching was much in evidence. In particular she made a practice of questioning each student in turn about his concept of God. Watching her mobile face, they could readily discern her pleasure when the answers more nearly measured up to her own spiritual comprehension of Deity, and the consequent change of expression when the replies fell short of the lofty standard so familiar to her exalted thought.

The answers given quickly indicated to Mrs. Eddy the points where clarification and instruction were most needed. Her own recognition and consciousness of the presence of God were so clear that it was with little difficulty that she was enabled to impart them to those prepared to receive and profit by her instruction, and it was largely on the basis of the realization of God as Love, that she healed the sick and taught her followers to heal.

Even apart from the content of her teaching, which can only

be indicated with extreme brevity at this point, there were other aspects of her approach which made for her success as a teacher and which endeared her to her students. One of these was her ready wit and the humor which often danced in her expressive eyes. While she could be stern when sternness was called for, she was ever ready to break the somber spell of undue seriousness with a jest or an amusing anecdote which, as every teacher would realize, often did more in making her point, than a series of sober explanations however logical.

Her sense of humanity was broad and compassionate. She understood and appreciated the efforts of her students to grasp her great subject, the Science of Christianity, and showed endless patience in clarifying, whether for many or even for one, points which appeared to need further explanation. Doubtless remembering the years during which she herself had sought earnestly to grasp the nature and implications of the revelation of this vast Science, she spared no effort in her eagerness to help others to do so.

Most characteristic of all her work and teaching was her constant reaching out for and remarkable response to divine inspiration. Her very humility, evident in everything she did, made it the more possible for her to attain to and profit by this spiritual sense, which was her guide at all times, and which she constantly commended to her pupils.

Mary Baker Eddy taught her students far more than mere doctrine, for the understanding which she imparted had a definitely practical end in view—that of healing the sick and reforming the sinner. Moreover, she was ever eager to have her students learn progressively to overcome inharmony under whatever guise it might appear.

Healing and teaching were in her thought inextricably connected, as they were in the thought of the Way-shower himself, Christ Jesus, to whom she constantly appealed in support of her work, which so signally fulfilled his demands upon his followers in every age. Mrs. Eddy considered healing as the very foundation of the Science of Christianity and made it plain that unless healing in its broadest sense resulted from the teaching which she, and in due course many of her students, gave, there must be something lacking either in the content or the method of the instruction given. So convinced was she of the naturalness and indeed the inevitability of healing on the basis of a growing understanding of God, that she saw this practical result as being more readily attained than success in teaching the great subject to which she had dedicated her life.

Nevertheless, there can be no question of the faithfulness and consecration with which she herself approached her educational work, and as a consequence, she was conspicuously successful in imparting to those who had the good fortune to study with her the meaning of Christian Science, so that they in turn could teach and prove their understanding by healing.

A most important step in the development of the educational system of Christian Science came with the founding by Mrs. Eddy of the Massachusetts Metaphysical College in January 1881, under a charter granted to her by the Commonwealth of Massachusetts. This College holds the unique distinction of being the only institution chartered for such a purpose under a state law (first passed in 1874 and repealed in 1882)—a law by which it is also permitted to grant degrees.

The College was situated originally at 8 Broad Street, in Lynn, Massachusetts. After August 1882, it was located at 569 Columbus Avenue, Boston; while after February 1884, its address was listed as 571 Columbus Avenue. It was carried on under the presidency and direct supervision of Mary Baker Eddy, and while she was assisted by six of her students who were named as Directors, actually all, or almost all, the work of teaching was done by Mrs. Eddy herself.

The College proved to be remarkably successful, and prepared more than four thousand students for the work of healing, and also for teaching in their turn, thereby contributing largely to the spread of the Christian Science movement. However, in October 1889, Mrs. Eddy decided to close the College at the height of its success, apparently feeling that for the time being its mission had been accomplished, and more especially because she wished to turn her undivided attention to the work of revising *Science and Health*.

No doubt some of her advanced students could have carried it on to some extent during her absence, but it had become increasingly apparent that those who came to the College for instruction did so with one primary object in view—that of studying with Mrs. Eddy herself. Since she felt the necessity of turning to other even more urgent work at this period, she clearly reasoned that it would be fairer for all concerned for her to close the institution altogether for a time. This would also have the effect of freeing the associate teachers for more direct attention to the ministry of healing.

Ten years later, in 1899, the College was reopened, still under the presidency of Mrs. Eddy, although by that time her work as Leader and Founder of what was already becoming a worldwide movement had grown to be so demanding that she now left the task of teaching to her students.

The previous year she had instituted the Christian Science Board of Education of The Mother Church, and the first Normal class for the training of teachers to be held under its auspices convened in January 1899.

The work of the Board of Education still continues under the provisions which Mrs. Eddy included in the Church Manual, Articles XXVIII, XXIX, and XXX. The Board consists of three members, a President and Vice-President who are selected annually, and a Teacher who is named triennially by The Christian Science Board of Directors. A Normal class, consisting of thirty pupils, is now held in Boston once in three years (counting from 1907) and is taught by the teacher designated to perform this important and responsible task.

Bearing in mind that the future of the Christian Science

movement lies so largely in the hands of such teachers, the selection of those who shall attend this advanced course, specially designed for the training of teachers of Christian Science, is made by The Christian Science Board of Directors with the greatest care, from the many qualified persons—either men or women—who apply. Their election is governed by various considerations. The applicants must have practiced Christian Science healing actively and successfully for at least three years, and must show evidence of their ability to profit by this specialized training, and of being outstandingly suited for the responsibility of teaching in their turn on the satisfactory completion of their course of study.

It is also stipulated in the *Manual of The Mother Church* (p. 90) that "All members of this class must be thorough English scholars." Thus this rule wisely applies not only to those students whose mother tongue is English, but also to those whose future teaching work will be carried on in other countries. While, as we have already noted, *Science and Health* has so far been translated into Dutch, French, German, Spanish and Swedish, it has been found advisable for all teachers of Christian Science to be fully familiar with our textbook in English—the language in which it was originally composed—thereby being in a position to impart to their students as nearly as possible the exact meaning which Mrs. Eddy intended to convey.

Yet another factor influencing the choice of students for the Normal class is a geographical one. Mrs. Eddy considered it important that teachers of Christian Science should be distributed throughout the world at key points where they could be readily reached by those who would in due course receive Primary instruction from them, since it is logical that such teachers should continue to carry on their work in the area in which they are already established and well known by their activity as Christian Science practitioners. This does not mean that a teacher is obligated to accept only pupils from his own

state or country, for many travel long distances to study with
the teacher of their choice.

By way of contrast, the reader may be interested to know that
those who attend the Normal class do not know in advance who
will conduct the sessions. This rule has the advantage of obviat-
ing any personal choice of teacher, thus centering the thought
of these advanced students upon the instruction given, rather
than upon the individual who gives it.

The course for training of teachers held under the auspices
of the Christian Science Board of Education is a thorough and
intensive one, covering not more than one week. Brief though
this period is, it may be borne in mind that the candidates
selected have already received Primary class instruction in Christian Science from an authorized teacher, while in addition to
the prescribed minimum of three years practical experience in
the work of healing, they have in most cases been earnest students of Christian Science for a much longer period.

While this triennial class for the preparation and qualification
of Christian Science teachers is vitally important, the basic reason
for its existence is to assure the perpetuation of correct and
authorized teaching of Christian Science throughout the world.
Thus what we call "class instruction" may be viewed as perhaps
the central point in the educational system of Christian Science.

Every authorized teacher of this subject holds a class of not
exceeding thirty pupils each year—the number being thus limited
so that as far as possible the members may receive individual
attention and instruction. Just as they themselves were carefully
selected before being admitted to the Normal Course held in
Boston, so these teachers have the privilege and responsibility
of choosing their own students from among those who apply to
them for instruction.

Teachers of Christian Science are not permitted to canvass
for students, nor to invite them to attend their classes. This
important step in the individual's progress in Christian Science
must be initiated by himself, and he is free to apply to any

teacher he may select. The significance which Mrs. Eddy herself attached to Primary class instruction is indicated by her rule forbidding any church member to advise against it. In selecting students, the teacher is governed by certain helpful rules laid down in the *Manual of The Mother Church* concerning the caliber of the applicants.

Class instruction, then, is a privilege available to those who have seriously begun the study of Christian Science, and having experienced some measure of its healing and regenerative effects, wish to enlarge their concept of its immense potentialities in meeting and overcoming all types of problems.

This period in the experience of a Christian Scientist is one which he anticipates with eager expectation, and recalls with the greatest joy and satisfaction.

As already indicated, each teacher conducts but one class a year. As stipulated in our *Church Manual,* the instruction is based directly upon the fourteenth chapter of the Christian Science textbook, entitled "Recapitulation."

The specific method and approach of each teacher of Christian Science is, of course, individual, but the over-all plan of all such instruction is surely to give the students a clearer and deeper understanding of the nature of God and of His creation, man, to clarify the vast significance of the revelation of Christian Science and its mission, and to stress the fundamental importance of Christ Jesus' ministry of teaching and healing with which it is so closely integrated.

These studies are also directed towards preparing the pupils not only for meeting their own needs and problems, but also for taking part in the wide ministry of healing to which every conscientious student of Christian Science is dedicated.

Indeed this Science in all its varied aspects, has a definitely practical objective—that of establishing healing and harmony and overcoming discord, limitation, sin and evil in every form. It is through the practice of Christian Science and the constant application of it in his daily experience that the student's progress is manifested and assured, and it is largely in this way that he gains an increased understanding of this subject and of the wideness of its possibilities.

Since *class instruction* is an individual matter, between the teacher and his own pupils, and since this privilege cannot be repeated except in the most exceptional circumstances, I can speak from personal experience only of the class which I myself attended, and which was conducted by Albert Field Gilmore, C.S.B., Litt.D.

Of the value to me of this period of instruction from an authorized and experienced teacher of Christian Science I cannot speak too highly. It brought into focus my own personal study of the subject, answered questions which, as a relatively new student, had been puzzling me, and brought me an even clearer assurance that Christian Science did indeed provide the answer to my needs and aspirations. It confirmed the stand I had taken in giving up what was regarded by my professors and my family as a promising theological career, and strengthened me in my conviction that I could contribute more to the general good as an active Christian Scientist than in any other way. This class study opened my thought to the wider implications of this subject and to its applicability to the practical solution of problems of all kinds. In short, the whole experience was one never to be forgotten and it constitutes a definite milestone along the path leading to my growing understanding of God, and of His constant and practical care for man.

Under the rules set forth in the *Manual of The Mother Church* the pupils of each teacher form themselves into an *association,* which naturally increases in number yearly, as long as the teacher's work continues. The association convenes once a year, and this meeting is designed to bring to every member renewed inspiration and further information along the lines of Christian Science. It is eagerly anticipated by students and teacher alike, and is a valuable and indeed necessary adjunct to class instruction.

The one which I myself attend annually meets in near-by New York City, but other regular attendants whom I know personally come for this single day, at their own expense, from many distant points, including California, Texas and Florida, and all parts of the United States, while one of the most faithful members of our group travels from as far afield as Australia, bearing witness to the importance which he, and other Christian Scientists, rightly attach to these association meetings.

The speaker on these occasions is normally the teacher himself, but the *Manual* makes provision for the continuation of such alumni meetings in the teacher's absence, by permitting the pupils to invite a consecrated and experienced student of Christian Science, who is in a position to do so, to conduct and address the annual meeting of their association. Consequently, the seed planted by class instruction is nurtured in its growth by such continuing yearly meetings, although the teacher may be no longer present in person.

In addition to the education provided for adults through class instruction, the Christian Science Church lays great stress on the training of its youth, and a highly important work is carried on by the *Sunday Schools* held under the auspices of The First Church of Christ, Scientist, in Boston, Massachusetts, and its branches throughout the world.

Young people are accepted for enrollment in our Sunday Schools up to the age of twenty, while in some instances the youngest class may include children of three or four years of age—the stress at this point being laid not so much on years, as on the ability of the child to grasp the simplest elements of Christian Science, which can form a basis for growing understanding of it. Many of our churches also have a nursery for still younger children. Not only does this make it possible for their parents to attend the church services regularly, but also provides a period in which the Christian Scientists in attendance can do their part in preparing these very young children for their Sunday School experience. In fact, in the church of which I am a member, young parents have repeatedly been heard to comment that our nursery furnished a determining factor in the choice of a location for their home.

In providing for Sunday School teaching, Mary Baker Eddy was clearly conscious of the necessity for Bible instruction, which meant so much to her in her own early training; and which she never forgot throughout her long career; while she also stressed the vital importance of introducing the children at an early age to the study and use of the Christian Science textbook. (See *Church Manual:* Article XX).

A vital part of the teaching in a Christian Science Sunday School deals with the impartation of a growing understanding of the nature of God. Even the youngest child readily grasps the thought of God as Love, while the teaching concerning the fatherhood and motherhood of Deity finds an equally ready response. It is the rule, rather than the exception, for the children in some of the youngest classes in a Christian Science Sunday School to be able to give, without a moment's hesitation, the seven basic names for God which Mrs. Eddy stresses—Mind, Spirit, Soul, Principle, Life, Truth, Love.

The children are encouraged to have and use their own books as soon as they can read, and in fact many of the tiny tots are eager to have their own textbook and Bible from which they "read" before they know what the pages actually say!

Among the earliest lessons which the children are taught come the Ten Commandments, the Beatitudes and the Lord's Prayer, together with its spiritual interpretation as given by Mary Baker Eddy (see pp. 68 f. above). As they grow up, these fundamental lessons are often reviewed to assure not only their familiarity with them, but also their growing understanding of their meaning. Throughout the teaching in a Christian Science Sunday School the question and answer method of instruction is widely used, and even at a relatively early stage attention is focussed upon the Lesson-Sermon studied by Christian Scientists through the week and read at our regular Sunday services. The extent to which this is used naturally depends somewhat upon the age-group.

Writing as one who has had the joyous privilege of teaching in various Christian Science Sunday Schools over many years, I have found it a highly rewarding and encouraging experience. The interest and alertness of these young people is both a challenge and an inspiration to the teacher. They early learn to practice what they are taught, and to apply Christian Science to the meeting of such problems as they encounter at home, in school and in college; not limiting their interest to what it can do for them, but extending it so that they can learn more of this essentially practical religion with a view to helping others, and improving the world in which they live. Often even the younger children, with the simple faith and ready acceptance of childhood, quickly grasp enough of the healing truth inherent in this study to be able to help their playmates, and also their parents, in times of difficulty, besides solving problems of their own.

From the very start, the children are taught that Christian Science is practical, something they can use at any time and anywhere, and this forms a firm basis for their future study and development. They soon come to recognize this Science as a way of life, a natural and essential part of all their activities, and, as a consequence, enrollment in Sunday School is—certainly in most cases—a matter of individual choice, rather than something expected or demanded of the children by their elders.

It may be added that the increasing attendance at our Sunday Schools and vital interest in them on the part of the pupils, arise spontaneously. They come because they enjoy coming. Picnics, entertainment, handcrafts, prizes, and so forth, are not employed in connection with Christian Science Sunday Schools. Their attraction lies solely in the instruction which they offer from the Bible and the Christian Science textbook, setting forth the true nature of God and of man and the results which flow in every

direction from an increasingly conscious recognition of this relationship—including progress, unfoldment, healing and enlightenment.

A word may be said at this point about the "Order of Exercises" in each Christian Science Sunday School. These exercises,
outlined in the *Manual of The Mother Church,* present in
abbreviated form, some of the main points in the regular order
of our Sunday church services, already described.

All the classes join in singing an opening hymn from the
Christian Science Hymnal. The Superintendent announces the
subject of the Lesson-Sermon, and the Golden Text—repeated
by the children—is followed by the Responsive Reading. Then
comes a brief period of silent prayer, and the repetition of the
Lord's Prayer in unison.

Following the period devoted to teaching in each individual
class, the session concludes with the reading of the *scientific
statement of being* by the Superintendent, and the singing of
another hymn.

A question sometimes asked by inquirers into the educational
system of the Christian Science church, is whether it supports
any denominational schools or colleges in addition to its Sunday
Schools, which, of course, form an integral part of The Mother
Church, and of each branch Church of Christ, Scientist.

In reply, it may be said that Mrs. Eddy established the Massachusetts Metaphysical College in 1881. It was not a college as
that term is usually understood. It was chartered for the purpose
of teaching Christian Science, and it now functions through
the Board of Education of The First Church of Christ, Scientist,
in Boston, Massachusetts. To attend a Normal class, one must
have been identified with the Christian Science movement in
the capacity of practitioner for several years, and have had
Primary class instruction with an authorized teacher. There are
no secular schools or colleges conducted under the auspices of
this church.

However, it is only fair to add that Christian Scientists value advanced education, and they join with other parents in their desire for the highest academic attainment for their children, and will be found supporting this opportunity for all students everywhere.

There are several fine, accredited educational institutions both in this country and abroad, which, although operated independently and without any official connection with our denomination, have been organized by Christian Scientists, and whose teachers and instructors are either exclusively, or at least primarily, active members of our church.

It is not the function of these institutions to teach Christian Science, and they scrupulously avoid trespassing in any way upon the work of our Sunday Schools, or on that of authorized teachers of Christian Science. Their importance, as I see it, lies largely in the fact that they provide for the children of Christian Scientists an opportunity for pursuing their secular studies in an atmosphere which does not conflict with their home training.

Space permits the naming of but two of these schools, both of which are co-educational: *The Daycroft School,* partly because it is situated near Stamford, Connecticut, only a few miles from my home, and I have visited it on various occasions, observing at first-hand the fine work it is doing; and *The Principia* in St. Louis, Missouri, because it is, I believe, the oldest, largest and most widely known of such schools.

The Principia was founded by a Christian Scientist, Mary Kimball Morgan, sixty years ago. Feeling the need of a satisfactory elementary school for her own children and for those of some of her friends who were also students of Christian Science, Mrs. Morgan opened what she called "The Principia" with sixteen children. Even in those early days its educational standards were high, and they have consistently remained so during the more than half a century of continued growth and activity of this "idea in action." Ever since its inception in 1898, the school has been staffed by active Christian Scientists and has retained its policy of enrolling young Christian Scientists as students.

Some idea of its growth and development may be gained from the fact that from the original sixteen, the enrollment had reached well over a thousand by 1957. The activities of *The Principia* have expanded over the same period so that it now offers a complete and carefully integrated curriculum extending all the way from Nursery School through four years of a Liberal Arts College. Where, originally, its few children were taught in a small rented building in St. Louis, there is now a campus of some ten acres within the city limits, while the college campus of 2,500 acres is situated in Elsah, Illinois, about forty miles distant. Further property of 366 acres has also been acquired for the new Upper and Lower School buildings now partially completed.

Impressive as these statistics undoubtedly are, the real work and success of *The Principia* are of far greater significance. In no instance is Christian Science taught in its classes, nor is there any effort made to interpret its academic subjects in the light of our denominational tenets. However, the very fact that both pupils and teachers are students of Christian Science results in their applying its practical teachings to the successful development of *Principia's* educational program, as well as to the growth of the individual.

Although the curriculum is wide and varied, stress is laid not so much on what the individual elects to study, as upon the constructive and effective manner in which he studies it. A consistent effort is made to broaden the students' approach to the democratic way of life, and to have them bear in mind the goal of contributing to the betterment of humanity, rather than concentrating on personal success.

In concluding this chapter, still another activity founded in 1946 for the benefit of young Christian Scientists, may be briefly mentioned: *The Christian Science Monitor Youth Forums,* which are also largely educational in their scope and purpose.

It is true of the Youth Forums, as it is of *The Principia,* that they are not official activities of The Mother Church, however these Forums, as their full name implies, find their focal point in *The Christian Science Monitor,* which provides the basis and inspiration for their discussions of current topics and their interest in constructive activities of young people in many lands.

One of their most interesting aspects is seen in their sponsorship of what are called "Travelships." These travel scholarships help to make it possible for Forum members in different parts of the world to visit other countries, acting as goodwill ambassadors, and contributing to the cause of international understanding.

The more than six hundred Christian Science Monitor Youth and Junior Forum groups now established in twenty-one countries, provide for wholesome and normal social and dramatic activities among their members, in addition to their primary object of contributing to the support and understanding of the *Monitor* and its wealth of many-sided and constructive information, which adds breadth to their educational development and good citizenship.

One of their most interesting aspects is seen in their sponsorship of what are called "Travelships". These travel scholarships

ELEVEN

CHRISTIAN SCIENCE AND THE BIBLE

IT HAS sometimes been suggested by those completely unfamiliar with Christian Science that Christian Scientists either
ignore the Bible or that they have a Bible of their own. Actually,
nothing could be further from the facts. So far from being
ignored, the Bible constituted the fundamental source book of
the Founder of our denomination and is constantly used and
referred to by every sincere student of Christian Science.

Mary Baker Eddy herself makes almost innumerable references to her recognition of the supreme value of the Scriptures;
for example—"The Bible has been my only authority. I have
had no other guide in 'the straight and narrow way' of Truth."
(*Science and Health:* p. 126). *Science and Health with Key to
the Scriptures* was never even remotely intended by its author
to supersede the Old or the New Testament, or to be considered
as a second Bible. As its name suggests, it was designed to provide a Key to unlock the treasure house of truth which we know
as the Bible, making these treasures more readily available for
the encouragement and support of mankind.

From early childhood Mary Baker was an earnest student of
the Scriptures and in this she was fully upheld by her mother,

who encouraged her to turn to the pages of the Bible, not only for spiritual advancement, but also for healing. So the search which culminated in the discovery of Christian Science and the writing of *Science and Health* and her other works on the subject, had continued for many years.

It is surely significant that when Mary Baker Eddy discovered what she afterwards named *Christian Science,* this revelation came to her following her reading of a passage of Scripture—the account of Christ Jesus' healing of a palsied invalid. On studying this account, she herself was healed of the effects of a severe accident and from that moment on she sought to discover how and why she had received this cure, so that she might be enabled to grasp more fully the *modus operandi* of spiritual healing with a view to learning how to practice it herself and how to impart it to others.

It was thus her study of the Bible which started her on the road to Christian Science, but while in all her work, all her thinking, all her practice, she returned to the Bible again and again for inspiration, healing and enlightenment, no honest observer can overlook the fact that the Christianly scientific *rule* which she established and interpreted for mankind had not been previously discovered by any of the countless students of these same Scriptures in the centuries that had passed since they were recorded.

One might add that, in a sense, the validity of the Bible is proved by Christian Science, which demonstrates that the Scriptural promises and assurances, far from consisting of pious theories or restricted to a bygone age, are as active and effective now as they were in the days of the Hebrew prophets and of the Master and his apostles.

I believe that any open-minded reader of the Bible and of *Science and Health* would feel bound to admit that Christian Science is essentially based on the Scriptures and cannot be separated from them. Some might possibly dispute Mrs. Eddy's interpretation of certain Bible passages, but if her premises are once accepted, her conclusions are indisputable, showing that as she understood the Bible, her book was unquestionably based upon it.

As I see it, the strongest argument in favor of the approach to the Bible which Christian Science teaches, is the practical test of experience. Not only does it claim that Christ Jesus' commands as recorded in the Gospels are intended to be taken at their face value and that he expected his followers in all ages to heal the sick as well as preach the gospel, but it also shows the practicality of such commands by obeying them, thus bringing forth proofs; of sickness and sin overcome, of discord and lack replaced by harmony and success.

Jesus himself said, "By their fruits ye shall know them." The fruits produced by Christian Science in healthier, happier lives and in the joyous effective practice of this new-old religion in every walk of life, provide satisfactory evidence that its whole-hearted acceptance of the Scriptural demands, teachings and promises, is justified by its results.

Mrs. Eddy was convinced that a growing understanding of the nature of eternal Truth, God, as revealed throughout the Bible, and an increased acceptance of the oft-stated fact of man's intimate relationship to Him, could not fail to have far-reaching effects in every area of human activity and experience. She proved this for herself and encouraged her followers to do so, assuring them that the results of their work would furnish evidence of the great possibilities that begin to unfold as man seeks truly to understand his Maker.

We speak of *Science and Health* as the textbook of Christian Science and so indeed it is, but when it was being wrought out by its author her sole guide was the Bible, with its records of the life, work and thinking of patriarchs, prophets, apostles and many others, and above all of the Master-Christian, Christ Jesus.

Today's student of Christian Science has before him two fundamental textbooks—the one derived from the other—the Bible and *Science and Health* based upon it; Mrs. Eddy had but one, and under the guidance of divine revelation, she built the structure of Christian Science on this ageless Scriptural foundation.

Immediately following her first radiant glimpse of Christian Science and the healing associated with it, Mrs. Eddy turned her attention, long centered on the Bible, even more intently in that direction. Indeed throughout her long career the Bible was her constant companion and she urged her students to follow her example of studying it daily.

We may safely assume that one of Mrs. Eddy's reasons for selecting the Authorized or King James Version of the Bible as the translation to be used in Christian Science services in all English-speaking countries was that in her day it was by all odds the most widely used and generally accepted version of the Scriptures in English. Indeed it was for all practical purposes, the only one, while the history of Bible translation, which I have had occasion to study in considerable detail, indicates clearly that this version has contributed more to the enlightenment of men, and to the establishment and spread of religious freedom, than any other. Is it not significant that within a decade of its publication, the Pilgrim Fathers came to our shores in search of freedom to worship God?

Moreover, may it not have been the clarity of expression of the beloved King James Version—which the Founder of Christian Science was reading at the time when she received her first healing—that furnished the transparency through which the light of the eternal healing Christ, Truth, dawned upon her consciousness, changing the course not only of her own life, but of the lives of countless followers as they too have learned to glimpse that light.

In the eight decades since *Science and Health* was first published, and more especially in the half century since the passing of Mrs. Eddy herself, many excellent translations have appeared, but even the ever increasing and well deserved popularity of the Revised Standard Version has done little seriously to challenge the position so long held by the Authorized Version. There is no question but that this well-loved rendering, prepared by the King James translators, will continue to be used in Christian Science services, partly because it makes for uniformity in the constructive sense of the term, assuring that the same Christian Science Lesson-Sermon can be read on any given Sunday wherever Christian Science services are held—and that means in all parts of the world.

Even when our services are conducted in some language other than English, the Bible translations used conform as nearly as possible to the thought and diction of the Authorized Version. It may be added that, as a rule, an English service is held in addition to the one conducted in French, German, Spanish or whatever the other language may be.

A further logical reason for our consistent use of the Authorized Version in our services is that to the large majority of visitors or casual attendants, the King James translation is already familiar, and thus provides the introduction to what may well be the less familiar words and thoughts of the Christian Science textbook —although, actually, as we see it, the two books are entirely consonant with one another. As I have indicated, *Science and Health,* far from neglecting or ignoring the Bible promises, takes them seriously and proceeds to show how the wonders and healings of Bible times can be repeated today by those who are willing to follow the Scriptural commands and examples by consistently applying the specific rules for Christian healing which the Discoverer and Founder of Christian Science was divinely inspired to set forth in her textbook.

In lecturing on the Bible, and referring to the King James translation in particular, I have often used this illustration:— The Authorized Version is like home to most of us; it is our headquarters, the base and center from which we work. Just as it is natural and beneficial that we should visit friends in other cities, other countries, upon occasion, so it is often helpful and inspiring to study other Bible translations from time to time; but our visits are rarely, if ever, permanent, for we return home.

Refreshed after such vacation periods, with no doubt a broader outlook than we had before, we are apt to feel a deeper appreciation of that home from which our journeyings began.

I believe it would be safe to assume that at least a majority of Protestants, whether or not they are students of Christian Science, are thus inclined to return to the Authorized Version as their base of operations, however much they may and do learn from the recent outstanding Revised Standard Version, or from the excellent translations of individual scholars, James Moffatt, Edgar J. Goodspeed and others.

While it has been my experience that Christian Scientists uniformly feel, as did their Leader, Mrs. Eddy, that the version which comes nearest to being a basic, generally-accepted English rendering of the Scriptures is that prepared in 1611 by the King James translators on the basis of the best manuscripts then available, let me again make it plain that this is said without any criticism of the many other renderings now in use, most of which I have studied, and each of which contributes its quota to an increased understanding and appreciation of the Book of Books.

Granted, then, that Mary Baker Eddy indicated clearly that she regarded the King James Version as the translation to be used in the conduct of Christian Science services, and also, by implication, as the primary one for use in the individual study of the members of her church, there is also ample evidence to prove that she herself did not use it exclusively in studying and clarifying the meaning of specific passages.

In her constant search for the original sense of the Scriptures, and above all for their spiritual import, Mrs. Eddy went back repeatedly to the original languages and also consulted what, in her time, were unquestionably "modern versions."

For example, she quotes directly from a translation prepared by the Rev. George R. Noyes, D.D., a noted scholar who was Professor of Hebrew and Lecturer in Biblical History at Harvard University, and brought out his version of the New Testament in 1869, just three years after Mrs. Eddy discovered Christian Science. She also quotes from the translation of Joseph Bryant Rotherham, who published his New Testament in England in 1872, followed a few years later by a rendering of the Old. Then, too, Mrs. Eddy has no hesitation in clarifying the sense of a passage in Genesis by reference to Dr. James Smith's well-known Bible Dictionary.

In view of these and similar passages, it is but natural that Christian Scientists feel free to follow her example by making use of current translations and reference works in the course of their individual study and efforts to grasp the true intent and significance of Bible passages, especially when they appear to be somewhat obscure as translated in the familiar Authorized Version.

One of the most conspicuous examples of Mrs. Eddy's periodic use of passages drawn from some translation other than the King James Version is to be seen on the cover of every copy of *Science and Health* and of her other writings and on other official publications of The Christian Science Publishing Society. This familiar seal or emblem, showing the Cross and Crown surrounded by part of a verse from the Bible, is registered as a trademark in the United States Patent Office and permanently identifies authorized Christian Science literature.

In selecting the text to be used for this important purpose, Mrs. Eddy turned to Matthew 10:8, but instead of the familiar wording of the Authorized Version she chose the rendering favored by the American Standard and English Revised Versions.

The words as used in this trademark are: "Heal the sick   Raise the dead   Cleanse the lepers   Cast out demons," where the Authorized Version reads "devils." Incidentally, *demons* is generally considered a more accurate representation of the term found in the original Greek. The variation is, perhaps, a minor one, but it provides an illustration of Mrs. Eddy's earnest desire to bring out as accurately as possible the meaning of any passage, whether or not the wording were strictly in accord with that of the King James translation.

Then, too, when Mrs. Eddy chose the text which appears at the head of the final page of every issue of *The Christian Science Monitor,* she did not select the phraseology of the Authorized Version. The words, "First the blade, then the ear, then the full grain in the ear," (Mark 4:28), appear both in the American Standard and in Dr. Ferrar Fenton's translation which was widely read in Mrs. Eddy's day, and with which she appears to have been familiar. It will be recalled that at this point the King James translators have: "First the blade, then the ear, after that the full corn in the ear."

When the Authorized Version was prepared in England in the early seventeenth century, "corn" was employed in the wide sense of grain of any kind—as it still is in British usage; while in American idiom it generally implies only Indian corn or maize, which was by no means intended when Christ Jesus gave this illustration of resistless growth and progress. Here, then, is a further instance in which a rendering was chosen evidently with a view to conveying a meaning which could not be misconstrued by the reader of our international daily newspaper.

Variant translations such as these could readily be used in such cases, when a single and more or less isolated passage was under consideration, but for over-all use, as I have indicated, the Authorized Version was retained and commended by the Discoverer of Christian Science.

TWELVE

ANCESTRY, EARLY TRAINING AND MARRIAGE OF MARY BAKER EDDY

MARY MORSE BAKER, was born on her father's farm in Bow, New Hampshire, on July 16, 1821. She was of Scottish and English descent, for her great-grandfather on her father's side, John McNeil, was a member of an old covenanting family in Edinburgh, and she may well have inherited from him that deep sense of independence and religious liberty associated with the Scottish Covenanters, and which, whatever its source, was clearly perpetuated in her life and work. John McNeil's daughter Marion married an Englishman, Joseph Baker and together they came to America in search of religious freedom, settling in New England.

Their son Mark, Mary's father, owned jointly with his brother James, a sizable farm of some 500 acres and the Baker homestead stood on rising ground overlooking the Merrimac river valley. Bow was a country township—a group of more or less scattered farms—rather than a town in the usual sense, but being only about five miles from Concord, the capital of the state, it was not unduly isolated, and churches and schools were near by.

Mark Baker was widely known and respected in his own and neighboring communities and took an active part in their affairs.

He was a Justice of the Peace and Sunday School superintendent of the local Congregational church and held various responsible posts in a regiment of the State Militia, occasionally acting as its chaplain. He was a deeply religious man, although somewhat stern and Calvinistic in his convictions, and, like my own father, daily conducted morning and evening prayers in his home.

Mary's mother, Abigail Ambrose Baker, although as religious as her husband, was gentler and more understanding. Her family, likewise of well-known and respected pioneer stock, came from the neighboring town of Pembroke, where her father was a pillar of the church, so much so that it was popularly known as the "Ambrose" church. Mrs. Baker was a person in her own right, who possessed considerable independence of spirit in her quiet way. In spite of managing a farm household and raising six children, she contrived to read quite extensively and her conversation and opinions, as well as those of her husband, were listened to with interest and profit by the many visitors to the Baker homestead at Bow.

Mary, the youngest child, was considered delicate, and was looked after by all with special care, although they could not be expected to foresee that this frail infant, born on a New England farm, was eventually to become known as a benefactor to the human race, and one of the most outstanding women of all time. However, even before Mary's birth, her spiritually-minded mother had an intuition, which she confided to an understanding neighbor, that the child she was about to bear had a career of deep importance awaiting her.

In due course Mary attended the country school about a mile distant, until the family doctor recommended that she be taught at home. Actually this did not interfere with her education, for she was naturally studious, reading avidly any books she could obtain; while soon her favorite brother Albert, eleven years her senior, took her under his special care. It was largely to his encouragement and ability in teaching that she owed her early training—unusually wide for a girl, especially a girl of her years, in New Hampshire at that period.

Because of Albert's strong and constructive influence on Mary during these impressionable years, a word may be said about his character and career. He was widely considered a young man of unusual promise and ability. At 20 he entered Dartmouth College, proving his scholastic prowess by being elected to Phi Beta Kappa before his graduation. He studied law under the tutelage of the Honorable Franklin Pierce, who later became President of the United States; in fact, Baker succeeded to Pierce's law practice. At 29 he became a member of the New Hampshire legislature, to which he was twice re-elected, and when he passed on just two years later, both friends and political opponents commended the brilliance of his intellect, and the consistency of his stand for what he felt to be just and right.

Such was the brother to whom Mary turned instinctively for support, understanding and instruction, which he freely gave; indeed the bond between brother and sister was remarkably close. He took seriously her intense desire for knowledge and did everything he could to encourage her literary aspirations.

Mary was but nine years old when Albert returned home from his first term at Dartmouth, but even then she confided to him her assurance that some day she would write a book and must begin to prepare herself for this task.

Recognizing her earnestness, he encouraged her to study both Latin and English grammar and during his vacations from his four-year college course, and later, when he was practicing law near-by, he introduced her to Latin, Greek and even Hebrew, subjects which added zest and understanding to her study of the Bible. We need not assume that Mary Baker made any deep or technical study of these languages, but there is sufficient evidence in her later writings to prove that she had at least a working knowledge of them, which, combined with her inspired intuition, enabled her to sense the deeper meanings which the Biblical writers strove to express.

In addition to these language studies, Albert introduced his sister to Natural Philosophy and Moral Science which formed a part of his college curriculum. By the age of ten, Mary had mastered the Westminster Shorter Catechism, following the custom of her Scottish ancestors—as I myself was required to memorize it at an early age. Mary's consistent study of Lindley Murray's *Grammar* and particularly of his *Reader*—justly popular in those days as providing an introduction to the works of Plato and Socrates, Marcus Aurelius and Cicero, together with Milton, Wordsworth, Addison, Pope, and many others—no doubt contributed to the development of the literary style for which, as the years went by, she was to become justifiably famous.

In short, it seems that like many young people who have been taught at home, or left to study for themselves, Mary Baker evinced a special interest in good literature which remained with her throughout her long career and is further shown by the many literary allusions in her writings.

Here, then, was a young girl with an insatiable desire for knowledge and the determination to obtain it, but letters dating from this period show equally plainly that hers was a normal, natural girlhood and that she enjoyed mingling with other young people of her age.

Turning to the religious side of Mary's upbringing, we find that her father was a firm believer in predestination. With this doctrine his quiet but spirited young daughter could not agree, in spite of her love for and loyalty to him. From her own study of the Bible she was already convinced of the unchanging love of God and could not accept the thought of His unconditional rejection of some of His children and the equally unconditional acceptance of others. To defend her position against the iron will of Mark Baker was a formidable task, but in so doing Mary proved her ability to uphold what she believed, a characteristic which stood her in good stead in later years when her faith in her great discovery, Christian Science, was to be constantly tested and as constantly maintained.

Mary's childhood stand took its toll in the form of a severe fever, but when at her mother's suggestion she turned to God in prayer, claiming the power of that divine Love which she had affirmed in her discussions with her father, she quickly gained her freedom, experiencing an early example of the Principle of healing which was to form the central factor in her life work.

This experience doubtless gave her support and encouragement in a further test which shortly faced her. At the age of 12 she received a preliminary examination for membership before the members of the Congregational church which her parents attended. Her replies to the opening questions were fully satisfactory, but when asked about predestination, Mary firmly declared that she could never believe in it, even if this meant her exclusion from membership. Impressed by her obvious sincerity and trust in God, both the minister and his congregation relented, and several years later she was accepted into their communion on her own terms, at the age of 17. Deeply appreciative of their understanding, she remained a member of the Congregational church until some fifty years later, when she founded a church of her own on the basis of Christian Science.

A further step in the development of Mary Baker's early life came with her marriage to Major George Washington Glover of Charleston, South Carolina, in December 1843, when she was twenty-two. It was a happy marriage, but within a few months, during a visit to Wilmington, North Carolina, on which his young wife accompanied him, he contracted yellow fever and passed on in a few days despite Mary's earnest prayers. It was typical of her that in spite of this tragic situation her first thoughts were for others. One of her first steps was to release her husband's slaves, which, as customary in the South at that period, constituted a considerable part of his property.

Brief though the period of her marriage with George Glover was, it had considerable bearing, as I see it, on Mary Baker's developing thought and on the preparation for her career. It gave her the practical opportunity to illustrate the concept of liberty so clearly shown in her later writings, by freeing her husband's slaves. Furthermore, we may surely assume that his sudden passing brought poignantly to her thought the ever-present need of realizing more fully God's healing power of which her mother used to speak and which she herself had already felt when in response to her childhood prayers her own fever vanished.

It was not long after Mrs. Glover returned to her girlhood home in New Hampshire that their child was born and named for his father, George Washington Glover II. In spite of her joy in her child, the experience of childbirth left her long a semi-invalid, until this and other physical difficulties were overcome at the time of her discovery of the efficacy of prayer alone as a powerful and practical method of healing.

Space does not permit any detailed discussion of the events of Mary Glover's life during the twenty-two years from the passing of her first husband in February 1844 to the discovery of Christian Science in February 1866, but a brief outline of these events, in so far as they cast light upon the development of her career, may be given here.

Because of the grave illness accompanying and following the birth of her son, she could not care for him herself. While appreciating the attention he received from others and under which he thrived, she could not but be troubled by the separation involved. Even when she grew stronger and was reunited for a period with her child, she was still considered too weak physically to raise him herself, and he was left largely to the care of a neighbor, while as the years went by this separation widened for various reasons, not attributable to his mother, thereby intensifying her loneliness. Still her indomitable spirit supported her in this time of stress.

Before her child was six years old, her own mother, to whom she had always been peculiarly close, passed on, while the following year her father married again. This placed Mary Glover in a difficult position. It was impractical for her to remain long under the roof of her stepmother, in spite of her kindliness, while the question of her financial support was also serious. Her husband's business had been successful, but crumbled when his guiding hand was removed and her stand in freeing his slaves had further depleted her slender resources. Such writing and teaching as she was strong enough to do at this time provided only a meager income for herself and her child.

At this juncture, Mary's sister Abigail, now Mrs. Tilton, offered her a home, but the Tiltons were unwilling to make room for her five-year-old son. In spite of her entreaties, the family decided that he should live with the nurse who had mothered him in babyhood and who was moving to a town forty miles away—not far in our day, but all too distant more than a century ago. As there appeared to be no alternative, Mary unwillingly accepted the plan, which increased the separation between her and her only child, whom she always loved dearly.

The significance of this development lies largely in the fact that it precipitated her second marriage, to Dr. Daniel Patterson, a dentist by profession and a relative of her stepmother. He expressed a deeply protective interest in the delicate and attractive young widow and before long succeeded in persuading her of his love. Moreover, he professed eager interest in the welfare of her son, craving the opportunity to help care for him and to give him a home. Above all, this turned the tide in his favor.

Mary Baker spent twenty years as Mrs. Patterson, and while she records his kindness to her and he in his turn bore witness to her purity and Christianity, it must have been a difficult period for them both. They lived briefly in various New Hampshire towns, although Dr. Patterson was often absent from home carrying on his widely scattered practice which became less and less lucrative as the years went by. Meanwhile his wife's physical difficulties which he had hoped to alleviate if not to cure through his care and his interest in homeopathy, deteriorated until she was bedridden a great part of the time. She herself tried various experimental methods of therapy current at that period, receiving occasional relief, but no permanent cure.

Through all these experiences, which sorely tried both her heart and her body, her courage and indomitable faith remained, and she continued her prayers and mental researches, hoping against hope that she would receive her answer. Little did she realize that when that answer came, as it did during this very period, it would not only bring her healing, but would enable and impel her to make the method of such healing available to countless thousands who have accepted it, and for all who are prepared to make it their own.

A few months following her discovery of Christian Science, Mary's husband deserted her, and eventually, in 1873, she was impelled to divorce him. Thus it was that when two years later her great work *Science and Health* first appeared, it was published under the name of Mary Baker Glover.

It was but natural that one possessing such a deep sense of mission and eagerness to help humanity as were characteristic of Mary Baker even in childhood, should crave the companionship and support of a husband fitted to understand and appreciate at least in some measure her exalted ideals and endeavors, especially now that the world-wide concept of Christian Science and its potentialities for good was gradually unfolding to her. Such a man was Asa Gilbert Eddy, who gave Mary Baker the name by which she is now known throughout the world.

Her brief marriage to Major Glover was both happy and successful. Her union with Daniel Patterson was prompted primarily by the hope, which proved to be unfounded, in spite of his apparent insistence that he would provide a home and fatherly care for her child. Even when that expectation proved fruitless, she did all possible to preserve the contract intact until he directly violated it.

Asa Gilbert Eddy, whom she married on New Year's Day, 1877, had an entirely different character from that of Dr. Patterson. Quiet, earnest, gentle and sincere, he had already wholeheartedly accepted the teachings of Christian Science and he performed many valuable services for his wife and for the Cause of Christian Science. For example, it was he who organized the first Christian Science Sunday School and played an important and active part in procuring the proper copyright protection for Mrs. Eddy's books. Mr. and Mrs. Eddy enjoyed a happy and fruitful companionship for five years, terminated by his sudden passing, apparently hastened by his grief at vicious and completely unfounded attacks against the integrity of his wife and of her work. His personal estimate of her career indicates by reflection something of his own character. "Mrs. Eddy's works," he wrote, "are the outgrowth of her life. I never knew so unselfish an individual, or one so tireless in what she considers her duty." (Wilbur: *Life of Mary Baker Eddy*: p. 266.)

It is completely typical of Mrs. Eddy that she did not allow her deep sense of personal loss resulting from the passing of this staunch Christian and Christian Scientist, her husband, to delay the prosecution of her appointed task, that of making Christian Science known to the world. Undaunted by this blow to her happiness, she was soon planning and publishing, at the age of 61, the first of the Christian Science Periodicals, then called the *Journal of Christian Science* and now known as *The Christian Science Journal*.

THIRTEEN

MARY BAKER EDDY:
DISCOVERER, FOUNDER AND LEADER

"IN THE YEAR 1866, I discovered the Christ Science or divine laws of Life, Truth, and Love, and named my discovery Christian Science. God had been graciously preparing me during many years for the reception of this final revelation of the absolute divine Principle of scientific mental healing." So writes Mary Baker Eddy on page 107 of *Science and Health*.

Her designation of Christian Science as a discovery, is highly significant, establishing the fact that this Science was in no sense an invention, but rather a revelation, an uncovering of the divine Principle which had always existed, awaiting recognition and acceptance.

One of the fundamental characteristics of Christian Science is its timelessness. The name by which we know it may date from the nineteenth century, but its effects extend back through the ages, and will continue to bring encouragement, enlightenment and true healing to future generations.

This is no mere personal evaluation, for this Science has proved its position and validity. It may be said without impropriety that, like the Christ, Truth, on which it is founded and which supplies its inspiration and authority, it is "the same yesterday, and to day, and for ever." As a system, it is new. As a fact, it is old.

The specific event in the experience of Mary Baker Eddy (or Mrs. Patterson, as she was at that time), which precipitated her discovery of Christian Science as a practical means of healing, occurred one cold February day some ninety years ago in the New England manufacturing town of Lynn, Massachusetts. She was on her way with a group of friends to attend a meeting of a local temperance society, when she suddenly slipped on the ice near the corner of Market and Oxford streets, and was thrown violently to the ground. Who could have supposed that this almost routine accident would eventually have even greater impact on the Science, Theology and Medicine of our era, than did the falling apple in young Isaac Newton's experience in establishing the concept of gravitation?—but so indeed it proved.

After a moment of shocked surprise, Mrs. Patterson's friends realized that this fall was more serious than they had supposed. Finding her to be unconscious, they carried her tenderly into a near-by house and called for a physician, whose very silence indicated the extreme gravity of the situation as he understood it. He later reported that he diagnosed the case as one of concussion of the brain, with possible dislocation of the spine. The following day she had partially regained consciousness and indicated her desire to be taken to her home in neighboring Swampscott. With considerable doubts as to the wisdom of such a move, considering her condition, her wishes were complied with. Two days later, on a Sunday morning, she called for her Bible, and re-read the account of the paralytic recorded in Matthew 9:2-8, which relates that although he had to be carried into Jesus' presence, he at once arose in response to the words of the great Physician, picked up the mattress on which he had lain and returned home, completely cured.

The Biblical account concludes with these words, ". . . when the multitudes saw it, they marvelled, and glorified God, which had given such power unto men." Can this not well be viewed as affirming the fact that such power, being God-bestowed, is ever available, as Mrs. Patterson proved it to be?

Her direct response to this cure of the paralytic, and the spiritual impetus which she gained from it, are best described in her own words: "As I read, the healing Truth dawned upon my sense; and the result was that I rose, dressed myself, and ever after was in better health than I had before enjoyed. That short experience included a glimpse of the great fact that I have since tried to make plain to others, namely, Life in and of Spirit; this Life being the sole reality of existence." (*Miscellaneous Writings:* p. 24).

How grateful Christian Scientists are—and all humanity might well be—that Mary Baker's spiritual sense was sufficiently attuned to reality, not only to catch this glimpse and to apply its meaning to her own need, but also that she had the vision to retain it in her consciousness—the unselfishness to spell out its meaning for all mankind in the Christian Science textbook! She did not claim that her understanding of this Science was fully developed at this moment of her own healing. There had been much conscious and unconscious preparatory work in her past experience, some nine years were to elapse before *Science and Health* appeared, but now she had seen her star, and had dedicated herself to follow its light wherever it might lead, and whatever difficulties or problems she might encounter along the way.

With a sense of deep humility, combined with a just recognition of the great destiny which had fallen to her lot, the Discoverer of Christian Science later wrote (*Science and Health:* p. 109): "For three years after my discovery, I sought the solution of this problem of Mind-healing, searched the Scriptures and read little else, kept aloof from society, and devoted time and energies to discovering a positive rule. The search was sweet, calm, and buoyant with hope, not selfish nor depressing. I knew the Principle of all harmonious Mind-action to be God, and that cures were produced in primitive Christian healing by holy, uplifting faith; but I must know the Science of this healing, and

I won my way to absolute conclusions through divine revelation, reason, and demonstration. The revelation of Truth in the understanding came to me gradually and apparently through divine power."

Mrs. Eddy's description of her experience at the time of her healing in Swampscott and of the progressive realization of the meaning of what she glimpsed in that moment, in terms of *revelation*, is highly significant, as I see it. It lifts her concept of the discovery into the realm of divine revelation. Both terms are important and stress different aspects of the same basic experience. From one side, Christian Science was *discovered* by her as the result or reward of her eager search; from the other, it was *revealed* to her through the power of God.

Mary Baker Eddy's discovery of the scientifically Christian way of life which she named *Christian Science* was indeed an event of the deepest significance. This is not only maintained by her followers, but is becoming increasingly apparent to the world at large as its results become more widely seen and felt, not only in their effects on individuals, but on society.

One of the essential reasons for the success and spread of Christian Science is to be found in the many steps which its Discoverer was led to take to ensure the establishment and progress of this highly productive idea—this sublime assurance that Christ Jesus' acts and promises were not out of date, but are as provable and practical in our age as they were in his.

Having once proved in her own experience that healing and enlightenment could replace sickness, accident, discouragement, as a consequence of earnest prayer to God and ready and confident acceptance of the teachings and practice of the Master Christian, she left no stone unturned in the effort to pursue this subject further, and to apply it in other directions. To change the metaphor, the inextinguishable light which had penetrated her thought that February day in 1866, when she received her first healing, was to grow ever brighter, irradiating her whole experience, illuminating the path which lay ahead and indicating countless ways in which her great discovery could be of service to mankind.

Important as was this discovery of Christian Science by Mary Baker Eddy, her self-imposed tasks of becoming both the Founder and the Leader of the Christian Science movement are of equal, if not of even greater significance. These developing activities serve to emphasize the caliber of her thought and the breadth and sweep of her truly selfless approach. The good she had personally received she wished to share, not only with her friends and neighbors, but with all who would listen—indeed with all mankind.

My object in the remainder of this chapter is to provide a brief résumé of my understanding of Mrs. Eddy's work as Founder and Leader, the magnitude of which appealed to me from the start—indicating some of the basic steps which she took in establishing Christian Science as an individual entity, in leading and guiding those who in due course became affiliated with it, and in organizing and maintaining a movement which is having an increasingly marked influence upon the religious and secular thought of our era.

Once the concept of Christian Science had dawned on her consciousness as a result of her own speedy recovery from the severe accident already described, followed by many months of prayerful study of the Bible and the nature of its application to the solution of human problems which corresponded to those of Christ Jesus' ministry—Mary Baker Eddy proceeded to put this Science into practice, not only on her own behalf, but on behalf of others.

The preparation and publication of her great work *Science and Health with Key to the Scriptures* provided further essential steps towards the fulfillment of her world mission. Her followers were growing in numbers, but lacked the cohesion which some form of organization could provide.

It is surely not without significance that it was on the Fourth of July, 1876—the one hundredth anniversary of the Declaration of Independence of the United States of America—that the initial steps were taken to establish what is now often referred to as the Christian Science movement, which offers to all men and has indeed brought to the many who, like myself, have been willing to accept its basic Principle, a sense of mental and physical freedom hitherto undreamed of, and above all, a clearer concept of God, a deeper realization of His presence and His power. In *Science and Health*, published just one year previously, Mrs. Eddy had written (page 106): "Like our nation, Christian Science has its Declaration of Independence. God has endowed man with inalienable rights, among which are self-government, reason, and conscience. Man is properly self-governed only when he is guided rightly and governed by his Maker, divine Truth and Love."

On that July day in 1876, Mrs. Eddy organized in Lynn, Massachusetts, a group of six of her students under the name of the Christian Scientist Association, and from this small beginning there gradually evolved the distinctive type of church government which is now in effect and which will be described shortly. Three years later, the Association concurred in Mrs. Eddy's thought that the time had come to found a separate church group, and forthwith the decision was made to organize a church established not only on the words, but also on the works of Christ Jesus. It should be noted here that the establishment of the Christian Science Church was in no way intended simply to originate one more religious sect, for no human organization of itself, ever effected salvation for mankind. This church, it was decided, would have no formal creed, and would be called the Church of Christ, Scientist, the first of its kind ever to be organized, while its unique mission and purpose would be to renew for mankind the hope, long since lost, of salvation from ills of the body as well as from sin.

This church was formally chartered by the Commonwealth of Massachusetts in 1879, and for a number of years it grew and prospered under the protection of state law, providing a rallying point for those early students who hailed Mary Baker Eddy as their Leader and accepted her interpretation of primitive Christianity. However, the very charter which acknowledged "the Church of Christ (Scientist)" as "an existing corporation" and gave it certain "powers, rights, and privileges," also stated that it was "subject to the limitations, duties, and restrictions which by law appertain thereto." (See *The Christian Science Journal*: Vol. XL; pp. 1-7).

In *Science and Health* (p. 583), Mrs. Eddy sets forth a brief but comprehensive definition of *Church*, indicating its spiritual mission as she understood it. Her words are as follows:— "CHURCH. The structure of Truth and Love; whatever rests upon and proceeds from divine Principle.

"The Church is that institution, which affords proof of its utility and is found elevating the race, rousing the dormant understanding from material beliefs to the apprehension of spiritual ideas and the demonstration of divine Science, thereby casting out devils, or error, and healing the sick."

In the light of this definition, it is by no means surprising that it became increasingly apparent to Mrs. Eddy that the advantages of a permanent state charter were overruled by the potential limitations involved. While helpful in the incipient stages of her church, the charter, if retained, might well restrict the taking of certain steps which she felt impelled to take as a result of prayerful consideration. This in no way implies that such steps would be in any respect illegal, or harmful to the state, although they might not conform to the technicalities of existing corporation law.

A further point regarding the inadvisability of continuing to carry on her church under the charter of *any* state, is seen in the fact that Mrs. Eddy was already envisioning the organization she founded as world-wide, reaching far beyond the boundaries of Massachusetts and indeed of the United States. Moreover, she saw that the Church of Christ, Scientist, was essentially a spiritual entity, subject to the laws and government of God, the one divine Mind.

Thus it was that in the year 1889, Mary Baker Eddy recommended, and the then members of the Church of Christ, (Scientist), unanimously voted, that they should dissolve their organization as originally constituted. While its charter as a corporation was thus abandoned, its name was retained and its ideals remained as firmly established as ever. Its influence continued to grow, and its adherents steadily increased in number.

In 1892 came another highly significant step in the organization of the Christian Science Church, placing it on a clearly defined and permanent basis. The state charter originally obtained and later abandoned as we have seen, stipulated that the church be established in—and by implication, limited to—Boston. Realizing ever more clearly the scope of the church she had founded, Mrs. Eddy now visualized it as a central or "mother" church, which, although having its headquarters in Boston, would be in no way limited to that city, but would draw its membership from students of Christian Science throughout the world. It was on this basis, therefore, that she reorganized her church under the title which it still bears—The Mother Church, The First Church of Christ, Scientist, in Boston, Massachusetts.

Under Mrs. Eddy's advice and direction, twelve of her students met at this time to put this organization into effect and became the original members of The Mother Church.

For some time the Leader of the movement and her followers had been contemplating the building of an actual church structure, and these plans received a new impetus with the establishment of The Mother Church.

Since 1886, some of the students had been endeavoring to secure a plot of ground on Falmouth Street, in the Back Bay section of Boston, but had been unable to complete the purchase. In order to secure it for the use of her church, Mrs. Eddy herself bought the property, and in 1892 she proceeded to convey it to a group of four Trustees who agreed to build there a suitable church edifice at a cost of not less than $50,000. Under a rarely used statute, she was enabled to effect this transaction and assure that her church should have permanent possession of the property, then valued at $20,000, although the Church of Christ, Scientist, no longer retained a state charter.

In the Deed of Trust conveying the land, Mrs. Eddy named the trustees "The Christian Science Board of Directors," who were to form a self-perpetuating body; and this Board still remains the governing body of The Mother Church. Under the *Manual of The Mother Church* which was written by Mrs. Eddy and sets forth the fundamental and irrevocable constitution and By-Laws of that church, the number of the Directors was later increased to five. They have the responsibility not only of administering the far-flung affairs of our church, but also of supporting and enforcing the rules laid down in the *Manual,* and their consistent devotion and loyalty to these tasks, and to the Cause of Christian Science, earn the gratitude and support of all loyal members of The Mother Church in this and other lands.

The task of planning and erecting the structure of The Mother Church went steadily forward and contributions poured in from Christian Scientists throughout the field. By the close of 1894, the building was completed in time for a joyous Communion service on the 30th of December, in spite of many delays and problems arising during the work of construction. One week later, on January 6, 1895, it was dedicated free of debt, and still stands, a monument to the courage and vision of the Discoverer and Founder of Christian Science.

The spiritual entity which we call "The Mother Church," now had a home of its own and its membership continued to increase in numbers, drawing upon students of Christian Science in all parts of the globe, whose loyalty to and gratitude for The Mother Church of their denomination is unbounded.

I can say from my own experience that membership in The Mother Church, The First Church of Christ, Scientist, in Boston,

Massachusetts, is both an inspiration and a support to the Christian Scientist. No matter where he may be, it provides him with a direct and vital contact with the headquarters of his chosen denomination.

I use the term *chosen* advisedly, for it has been my observation that many more people become students of Christian Science by choice and conviction, as I did myself, than inherit it as a legacy from their parents. Even those who have been raised from infancy to learn and profit by this truly practical way of life, generally discover that they must find it for themselves, and make it their own, before they can recognize and properly evaluate the tremendous potentialities for good, health, progress and spiritual unfoldment which are available to them through this study. Membership in The Mother Church—open to applicants from the age of twelve—is a great step towards this realization, whether on the part of the convert or the one who has known of Christian Science from early childhood.

The very phrase "The Mother Church" naturally suggests that it must have offspring—and so indeed it has. These "branches," as they are called, over three thousand of which are to be found in this and other lands, form an important and indeed an essential part of the organization of the Church of Christ, Scientist, as Mary Baker Eddy envisioned and established it.

Each branch Church of Christ, Scientist, is an independent, self-governing body with its own local membership. It is essentially democratic in its church government, and prepares its own By-Laws. These By-Laws could not logically be contrary to The Mother Church *Manual*, while on the other hand, they must not duplicate it. They provide for the organization and orderly government of the corporate body under its charter, and according to civil law, wherever the branch church is situated. Its members elect a rotating board of directors, or of trustees, to hold general management over its church affairs. The two Readers who conduct its services are also elected directly by the membership from among their own number.

The fact that under the By-Laws of the *Manual of The Mother Church* the Readers in every branch church, as well as those in The Mother Church itself, must be members of The Mother Church in Boston, and so subject to the rules contained in the *Manual,* is one of the very few mandatory links between The Mother Church and its branches. In actual practice, however, the relationship is remarkably close, although The Mother Church is most careful not in any way to enforce its will upon the local branches, which are free to act independently as the conscience of their members and the needs of their communities may direct.

The bond between The Mother Church and its branches is not dissimilar, as I see it, to the intimate relation of the United States, each with its individual authority and self-government, to the Federal government centered in Washington. The very independence of the Christian Science branch churches unites them more fully and firmly to The Mother Church, indeed in the great majority of cases, active members of a branch church are also members of The Mother Church. This organizational system, unique in the ecclesiastical field, has been found to be both practical in operation and helpful to all concerned.

It may be added that in addition to its branch churches, our church also recognizes Christian Science *societies*—small groups of active students of this subject not yet sufficiently organized to qualify as branch churches. Then, too, bearing in mind the needs of our young people attending universities and colleges, provision has been made for the formation at most larger colleges in the United States and abroad, of Christian Science *organizations,* which hold informal meetings, to which both faculty and students are welcome.

The original edifice of The Mother Church, dedicated as we have seen, in 1895, seats just under one thousand, and before many years had passed it became increasingly evident, both to Mrs. Eddy and to the rapidly growing membership of her church, drawn from all parts of the world, that an additional and much larger building would have to be constructed. The first direct step in this direction was taken at the Annual Meeting of the Mother Church in June 1902, when the members gathered in Boston at that time, ten thousand strong, pledged for themselves and for some fourteen thousand not present, to raise up to two million dollars for the erection of what was later to be known as the Extension of The Mother Church.

Within ten months, the necessary ground in the immediate vicinity of the original edifice had been acquired—no small achievement when we consider that this involved the negotiation for and purchase of ten separate lots. The story of the planning and erection of the building itself is an inspiring one, which cannot be discussed here, but the interested reader is referred to Margaret Williamson's *The Mother Church Extension,* which recounts in vivid detail the progress and fulfillment of this great project. By June 1906 the Extension was ready for dedication and the many thousands who gathered for the Annual Meeting rejoiced not only in the beauty of the edifice itself, but in hearing the confirmation of an announcement made the previous week that the building fund was now closed, as the building was completely paid for. (It may be added that all Christian Science churches adhere to this practice of not dedicating their structures until they are entirely free of debt.)

Built of Indiana limestone, the Extension of The Mother Church, seating approximately 5,000 people, adjoins and is directly connected with the Original Mother Church; and its dome, reaching to a height of more than 200 feet above the level of the pavement, forms a familiar landmark in the Back Bay section of Boston. One of the noteworthy features of the interior of the Extension is its four-manual organ, one of the largest in the Western Hemisphere.

Near by is to be found the headquarters of The Christian Science Publishing Society, now located in a building completed in 1934, which houses, in addition to editorial and other offices, a modern and complete plant for the printing and publishing of Christian Science literature, including *The Christian Science Monitor*.

From the early days of the movement, the work of preparing and distributing such literature—some of which has already been described in Chapter Nine—was found to be of vital importance, and the space devoted to it had to be constantly expanded, culminating in the completion of the present ample building, as beautiful as it is practical. The previous Publishing House, across the street from the present structure, was remodelled to become the Administration Building, and now contains the offices of The Christian Science Board of Directors, and of other officials of The Mother Church.

The work of The Christian Science Publishing Society is under the supervision of a Board of Trustees, originally established by Mrs. Eddy in 1898.

Another distinctive aspect of the Christian Science church, which is closely connected with its organizational development, is to be seen in the activities of its *Committees on Publication* throughout the world. As the church she founded grew in numbers, and as a consequence was increasingly in the public eye, Mrs. Eddy's ever alert awareness of its needs and problems brought to her attention the fact that many misconceptions were apt to arise with regard to her church, misconceptions which could be readily and courteously corrected if there were individuals assigned to this task.

Under the provisions of the *Manual of The Mother Church*, The Christian Science Board of Directors elects annually, a loyal and capable Christian Scientist, a resident of Boston, to serve as a committee of one, and also to fulfill the important task of acting as manager of the widely scattered Committees on Publication at home and abroad. Each state in the United States has such a Committee (again consisting of one individual), and each county in Great Britain which warrants such representation has a Committee on Publication, as do the provinces of Canada,

and the states in Australia and South Africa. In other parts of
the world a country is usually represented by a Committee on
Publication, where the interest warrants. Then the various local
Committees have as a rule an assistant in each branch church in
their territory to aid in keeping them in close touch with the
various localities within the area lying under their jurisdiction.

The over-all duties of the various Christian Science Committees on Publication may well be said to lie primarily in the field
of Public Relations, since they are called upon to act as liaison
officers between our church and the general public. If a mis-
statement concerning the teachings or practice of Christian Science appears in the daily press, or in a book or periodical, and
it comes to his attention, it is the responsibility of the Committee
on Publication in that area to get in touch with the publisher
or author in a courteous and friendly manner and clarify the
point at issue. Many interesting and mutually helpful contacts
have thus been made. In most cases the cause of the misstate-
ment is found to be simply a misapprehension on the part of
the writer of what Christian Science really is, and the correction
or enlightenment is readily accepted. In other instances, a "Letter
to the Editor" prepared by the Committee has been found to
be an effective means of making such a correction.

Another aspect of the work of the Committees on Publication
is the close contact they maintain with the legislative bodies of
the various states, seeing to it that any pending legislation which
might adversely affect Christian Scientists or the practice of
Christian Science, is carefully studied, and that steps are taken,
wherever possible, to protect the rights and privileges of the
members of our church as citizens under the constitution of the
United States, or of other countries. In many instances such
activities succeed in preserving not only the freedom of our own
denomination, but also that of others, for the motive in all such
work is to aim for the establishment of what is right and fair
for every citizen.

The various local Committees on Publication often have the

privilege of addressing, by invitation, groups belonging to other churches, who wish to have a brief outline of what Christian Scientists believe and how they put their religion into practice. Such meetings also contribute to the end of correcting mistaken views about the nature and aims of Christian Science.

Most of the radio and television programs sponsored by The Mother Church are presented under the auspices of the Committees on Publication, and these programs, many of which include direct and personal statements made by those who have themselves experienced the practical results of Christian Science in overcoming moral, financial and physical problems of all kinds, have aroused increasingly wide attention among those who hear or see them.

From this brief outline of the activities of the Christian Science Committees on Publication, the reader may grasp something of the important work which they accomplish in connection with our denomination, as well as in contributing their part to the cause of religious freedom in general.

I cannot conclude this chapter without at least a passing reference to three outstanding Charitable Institutions, which, although partially self-supporting, are sponsored by The Mother Church and largely financed by it and by contributions from individual church members.

One of these is known as the Christian Science Benevolent Association Sanatorium in Chestnut Hill, Massachusetts, and its counterpart on the Pacific Coast is in San Francisco, California. Both are situated in spacious and beautiful grounds and are available for the use of guests receiving Christian Science treatment, and for others who come primarily for rest or study.

The third institution, The Christian Science Pleasant View Home, on the site of Mrs. Eddy's former home near Concord, New Hampshire, was primarily designed for the benefit of veteran Christian Scientists seeking a permanent place to live, and in which to continue their constructive work.

Thus it will be seen that once she had discovered Christian

Science and founded the world-wide movement based upon it,
Mrs. Eddy not only provided for its organization, development
and maintenance, but also left the way open for considering
the needs of the individual.

It is surely abundantly clear that Mary Baker Eddy, even apart
from her remarkable spiritual insight and courage, embodied
the elements of true leadership, for throughout her long career
she proved herself a true pioneer, ever alert to meet present
needs while building for the future. Never deified or worshipped,
she is nevertheless honored and beloved by her followers as in a
special and permanent sense their Leader—in following Christ
Jesus.

FOURTEEN

THE CHRISTIAN SCIENCE TEXTBOOK

IN APPROACHING the study of any important subject, the sincere student naturally seeks to procure for his instruction the best textbook available, prepared by an expert in his chosen field.

When turning his attention towards the Science of Christianity, he quickly finds that although much has been written about it, there is but one authentic and authoritative textbook of Christian Science Mind-healing. This book was written by Mary Baker Eddy herself, who, as both Discoverer and Founder of Christian Science, was uniquely fitted to set forth its basic teachings and the means of putting them to practical use.

In naming her book *Science and Health with Key to the Scriptures,* Mrs. Eddy indicates at the very outset, something of the scope and basis of her great discovery. We of the twentieth century live in an age of scientific research, and even in 1875, when *Science and Health* was first published, much attention was already being paid to the advances of science. However, as I understand the life and writings of this great religious leader, I cannot feel that she chose to include *Science* both in the title of her remarkable book and in the name of the faith she founded, with any intention of using the term merely to popularize or modernize her interpretation of Christianity. After all, *Science*, as we all know, is simply the English form of the Latin *scientia* —knowledge or wisdom. Christian Science may well be described as the practical interpretation and application of the Master's teachings, a demonstrable knowledge of their effectiveness present in human experience.

That Christ Jesus recognized the value of such knowledge, or science, is surely indicated in this familiar assurance: "If ye continue in my word, then are ye my disciples indeed; And ye shall know the truth, and the truth shall make you free." (John 8:31f.).

Mrs. Eddy's conjoining of *Science* and *Health* in the title of her textbook reminds us of her recognition of another primary aspect of the Master's mission to mankind. Not only did he see knowledge of the truth as a natural and necessary prelude to freedom, but also, throughout his ministry, we notice his deep preoccupation with health. To quote Peter's brief but vivid description of Jesus' career: he "went about doing good, and healing all that were oppressed of the devil; for God was with him." (Acts 10:38). He seems never to have lost an opportunity of healing either individuals or multitudes, and was specific in his repeated commands that his followers also should "heal the sick."

The choice of the phrase "Science and Health" was not made lightly. It came only after much prayerful thought, and as a result of what Mrs. Eddy reverently regarded as divine revelation. Even to a newcomer, it provides a provocative title, while the more one studies the textbook of Christian Science, the more he finds that it can indeed bring him both *Science* or *Knowledge* of the truth of being on which Christianity is founded, and a renewed sense of *health* and well-being.

"Six weeks I waited on God to suggest a name for the book I had been writing," Mrs. Eddy records. "Its title, Science and Health, came to me in the silence of night, when the steadfast stars watched over the world,—when slumber had fled,—and I rose and recorded the hallowed suggestion." (*Message to The Mother Church, 1902:* p. 15). Undaunted by the attitude of some of her friends with whom she shared the experience, and who promptly advised her to forget this proposed title and even the book itself, she persisted in her work and in using the name which had come to her.

Months later her choice was upheld from an unexpected source—the Bible itself! A friend showed her an edition of Wyclif's famous rendering of the New Testament in which the phrase translated "knowledge of salvation" in the familiar words of the Authorized Version (Luke 1:77), appears as "science and health." While it is true that in most editions of Wyclif the phrase occurs as "science of health," I myself have examined copies in which the words "science and health" appear, as Mrs. Eddy brings out, thus confirming the title which came to her independently.

In selecting the final name for her book, Mary Baker Eddy added to "Science and Health" the words "with Key to the Scriptures." To many, the Bible has been to some extent a closed book, owing to failure to appreciate, in many instances, its spiritual meaning and the symbolism which it contains in numerous passages. Many of its treasures needed to be unlocked for the benefit of mankind, and towards the close of her book, Mrs. Eddy does indeed provide a key to the Scriptures, dealing primarily with two books of the Bible often misunderstood—Genesis and Revelation—and adding a Glossary of Scriptural terms, setting forth their spiritual meaning as she understood it. Actually, her whole work might justly be viewed as a *Key to the Scriptures,* for it brings to light so clearly the inner meaning of these sacred writings, together with their practical and perennial effectiveness.

The story of how this unique book, *Science and Health with Key to the Scriptures,* came to be written and of the vicissitudes through which it passed in its early years, until, today, its circu-

lation is second only to that of the Bible itself among books of
a serious character, is of deep interest, not only to Christian
Scientists, but also to others who wish to understand its nature
and its purpose. For this reason, I feel that it will be helpful
at this point to give at least the highlights of its beginning and
unfoldment.

Following her discovery of Christian Science in the year 1866,
Mary Baker Patterson—as she then was—encountered a series of
difficulties and disappointments which might well have dashed
the spirits of one less earnest and consecrated in her convictions.
In that very year, as we have seen, Dr. Patterson deserted her,
and eventually, in 1873—only a few months after her father's
passing—she felt impelled to divorce her husband. Then, while
her sister Abigail, with whom she had lived at one time, invited
her to return, it was on condition that she would renounce her
interest in healing by prayer. This condition Mary could never
accept. Inspired by her own healing, she was determined to discover the Principle which lay back of it, the means by which it
had been accomplished, so that she could share with others that
which had so greatly benefitted herself.

In many respects it was a deeply trying period, a wilderness
experience, but, as events proved, a highly profitable one, for
the enforced separation from family ties focussed her attention
ever more directly upon her true mission in life, that of establishing Christian Science. That this was no easy task can only be
imagined by the reader, for even when the undertaking is one
which repeats or follows a pattern established by others, there
are endless problems to be faced and solved. The Founder of
Christian Science, it must be remembered, was introducing a
new idea, a new concept, and one which the world would come
to regard as revolutionary. In this pioneer work she was moving
forward against the tide of centuries of resistance to any change
in the religious *status quo,* and nothing less than her trust in God
and her deep love for mankind could have made her great
accomplishment possible.

In thus introducing to mankind this mighty thesis of the power of the divine Mind in human affairs, she was aware of the possibility that some might seek to misuse this power for selfish or nefarious ends, but she felt impelled not to withhold her great discovery.

As we have seen, from this time forward she gave the most earnest attention to the study of the Bible, searching not only for the explanation of her own swift recovery, but also for the basic rule involved, so that its broader application might be understood by herself and eventually be made available to all the world.

Accepting wholeheartedly the Biblical assurance that man was made "in the image of God," she was equally convinced that His spiritual creation could not deteriorate, for would not man's Maker forever uphold the standard of perfection which He had originally established?

Sickness, disease and all inharmony were seen as having neither sanction nor support in the divine order of things. As these basic concepts of God-bestowed harmony and healing developed in her consciousness, she tested their validity by applying them to the physical and other problems which she encountered among her friends and neighbors, and, noting their effectiveness, she was encouraged in her never-ending search for more swift and effective proofs of the present-day results of Christian healing and regeneration. She found increasingly that she was able to impart at least some portion of her understanding of healing to others, who, in their turn, learned to put it into practice.

As her teaching work developed, it was but natural that she should feel the value and importance of recording her growing understanding of Christian Science, partly for the clarification of her own thought, and partly so that her students and those of the future would have a correct text to study, in addition to the Bible on which all her teaching was based.

Within four years after her own healing, Mrs. Glover, as she preferred to be called at this period, had prepared a brief pamphlet which she named "The Science of Man," providing a summary of the conclusions she had reached. Although copyrighted in 1870, it was not actually published until later, after the appearance of the first edition of *Science and Health*. During these intervening years, she copied out her manuscripts by hand and distributed them among her students.

The full title of "The Science of Man" as it appears on the title page of the original edition published in Lynn, Massachusetts in 1876, indicates its suitability for classroom use, and is of historical interest as showing some of the points which Mrs. Glover particularly stressed at this early period in her work: *The Science of Man, by Which the Sick are Healed, Embracing Questions and Answers in Moral Science. Arranged for the Learner by Mrs. Mary Baker Glover.* This *Science of Man* forms the basis of the chapter now entitled "Recapitulation" in *Science and Health*—a chapter which, in its turn, is the text used for Primary class instruction in Christian Science.

The writing of *Science and Health* itself covered a period of several years, which seems to have begun not long after its author's discovery of Christian Science in 1866. Even a brief perusal of its pages shows that it was not the kind of volume which could be written quickly. Despite its unquestioned Biblical basis, many of its propositions were to be considered startling, if not revolutionary, when it was eventually presented to the public, and its author was determined to weigh with the utmost care and to prove for herself each statement relating to the new-old Science of Christianity which she had discovered, and which constantly unfolded to her receptive thought. The task of writing *Science and Health* was a truly monumental one, but it proved to be deeply rewarding to its author, not only at the time of its preparation when the vision of her subject expanded into ever widening realms of constructive expression, but also in later years, for she lived to see her book bring inspiration, enlightenment and healing to uncounted thousands of readers.

By the year 1872, Mrs. Glover had an outline or prospectus

of her work sufficiently far advanced that she was prepared to submit it for the consideration of a publisher. About the same time, George Clark—the son of a woman with whom Mrs. Glover was boarding at the time—had completed a manuscript of his own, a racy tale of seafaring life, and they set out for Boston together, to offer their books to the same publisher. Clark's manuscript was readily accepted, but Mrs. Glover's was as definitely rejected, on the ground that it was thought to have no commercial possibilities; in fact, the editor advised her to abandon her work altogether. Undismayed by this rebuff, she rejoiced with her young friend in his success, and returned quietly to Lynn to continue her studies and to revise and expand her book.

As every experienced author knows, the original rejection of a cherished manuscript does not necessarily doom it to oblivion, but often paves the way for necessary revision and development, leading to its eventual success—and so it was in this case. For almost three more years Mary Baker Glover worked assiduously over her book, smoothing its forms of expression and clarifying its content. She lived at various different addresses in Lynn during this period, but the final touches were given to her manuscript in a home of her own which she had purchased at 8 Broad Street, although at this time her limited finances only permitted her to retain a part of the house for her personal use. Thus it was that a small garret room, with one skylight in the sloping roof, saw the completion of her work on the first edition of *Science and Health*.

At last it appeared in printed form on October 30, 1875, in a modest edition of one thousand copies, the cost being borne partly by the author and partly by two of her devoted students. Little could any of them realize that by 1906—thirty-one years later—the book would have passed through 418 editions! (After that date the editions were not specifically numbered.) During her lifetime, Mrs. Eddy constantly revised her great work, to assure the highest degree of clarity, accuracy and good English style. The basic substance, however, remained the same as in the

First Edition, although its form improved as a result of constant and consistent polishing, and the unfoldment of her ever-active thought. No changes have been made in *Science and Health* since her passing in December 1910.

To give a brief sketch of the content of the Christian Science textbook is an all but impossible task, if for no better reason than that the more than six hundred pages prepared by Mrs. Eddy cover such a wide range of subjects, such a broad array of enlightening and constructive ideas:—but at least an inkling of its scope can be indicated by mentioning the headings of its chapters. Over the period of some thirty years during which Mrs. Eddy herself was constantly studying and revising the successive editions of her great work, there were many changes in the order of the chapters as they appeared in the first edition, and considerable variation also in their titles, but, as I have already suggested, the basic substance and content remained the same.

In its final form, which has now been established for many years, and which, of course, Mrs. Eddy herself authorized, *Science and Health* consists of eighteen chapters and a preface.

As might be expected, the Preface of six pages tells how and why the book came to be written, and records something of the early progress of the Christian Science movement; while it also contains many indications of the great message to be presented in the book itself. One brief sentence from its opening page presents a challenge to the reader: "The time for thinkers has come." This does not imply that the book is hard to understand, but it clearly indicates that a thoughtful and open-minded approach to it, and to Christian Science itself, is essential, if one would appreciate their true significance. It certainly shows the vision of the author of the Christian Science textbook concerning the time in which she lived and the ages to come.

Together with countless students of this subject, Mrs. Eddy was correct in her evaluation of her book, and in recognizing the futility of anything less than thorough and continuing study in order to equip the inquirer even to judge it wisely, to say nothing of utilizing its teachings successfully.

Many readers have found that the opening chapter on "Prayer" was sufficient to assure them that the message of Christian Science was what they had long sought. This, for example, was my wife's experience; and further study only confirmed this assurance; while, as I have indicated, my own first study of this chapter a number of years earlier had much to do with my becoming a Christian Scientist.

The second chapter in *Science and Health* discusses "Atonement and Eucharist," explaining Mrs. Eddy's interpretation of these great facts as based on her understanding of the Bible. Next there follows a chapter on "Marriage," and another making it plain that Christian Science has no connection with spiritualism, reaffirming that God alone is Spirit, and in constant control of His universe.

The brief but powerful chapter which follows, entitled "Animal Magnetism Unmasked" shows that Mind's divine control cannot be subverted by mesmerism or hypnotism, (also known as "animal magnetism"), nor can it be influenced by astrology, all of which are the very reverse of Christian Science. Here Mrs. Eddy deals emphatically with criminal forces which, remaining unseen and unchecked, can undermine our highest ideals.

The sixth chapter of *Science and Health* discusses three important realms of current thought, "Science, Theology and Medicine," indicating how Christian Science, understood and practiced, achieves the ideals for which these systems strive. As might be expected, Mary Baker Eddy translated into their spiritual significance these three departments of service to humanity, and proceeded to show the impact upon them of the ever practical Science of Christianity which she discovered and made available to mankind.

In the next chapter, "Physiology," Mrs. Eddy makes it plain that a recognition of God's omnipotence and of the capabilities

of man as His reflection, is more effective in overcoming disease
than is physiology with all its alleged laws and arguments.

Having dealt with a number of systems and doctrines which,
as commonly accepted, are not consonant with Christian Science,
Mrs. Eddy now proceeds to introduce her readers to specific
instances of freedom, progress and healing, in a chapter called
"Footsteps of Truth," in the course of which she urges her readers to claim the intelligence conferred by the one Mind, God,
upon His spiritual reflection, man, renouncing at the same time
the false belief of Mind obtaining in, or subject to matter.

The following chapter, headed "Creation," develops this
thought still further, emphasizing the thesis that since infinite
Mind is none other than the creator of all, and creation constitutes the infinite outcome or idea proceeding from this Mind,
all true creation must be good and spiritual, by reason of its
perfect Source.

Chapter Ten, entitled "Science of Being," (and particularly
its concluding portion which gives the Platform of Christian
Science), is viewed by many students as the central portion of
this great book, in that it sets forth at some length the main
points of Christian Science, stressing the allness of God and the
nothingness of matter; while the next chapter, as its name—
"Some Objections Answered"—naturally indicates, replies to some
questions which may have entered the thought of the reader.

The next two chapters, entitled "Christian Science Practice"
and "Teaching Christian Science" respectively, provide cogent
and varied illustrations of the practical application of this Science to problems of various types, indicating also how this
subject should be gradually taught or explained to the inquirer.
Here it is shown that no matter how assiduously it is studied,
the mere letter without the acceptance of the spirit, is of little
value, while it is also made plain that if the student persists in
cultivating a truly spiritual and constructive approach, he can
be assured of enjoying what St. Paul describes as "the fruit of
the Spirit."

This section of *Science and Health* closes with a chapter on "Recapitulation"—a concise summary of the previous chapters, which, as we have seen, is used as the basis for teaching Primary classes on the subject of Christian Science.

Under the main heading "KEY TO THE SCRIPTURES" are to be found three chapters, giving examples of Scriptural interpretation in the light of Christian Science. The first deals with "Genesis," throwing further light upon the spiritual concept of creation already discussed in the chapter of that name. The second, entitled "The Apocalypse," elucidates the revelations which came to St. John at Patmos, while the third is a "Glossary" which interprets metaphysically many Bible terms. It may be added that their spiritual significance as defined in this chapter, often serves to clarify Scriptural passages which would otherwise appear puzzling or confusing.

The final chapter of *Science and Health,* headed "Fruitage," was not written by Mrs. Eddy herself, but is of interest in that it contains one hundred pages of carefully authenticated statements or testimonials by people from all walks of life who had obtained reformation or healing simply through reading or studying this remarkable book.

"Fruitage" first appeared as a part of *Science and Health* in 1902, after, with the permission of Mrs. Eddy, two of her faithful students, Mr. Edward A. Kimball and Rev. William P. McKenzie, had selected these testimonies from among thousands of letters of a similar character, indicating both the deep inspiration and the practical effectiveness of the Christian Science textbook.

This chapter would be in no way complete without some evaluation, however brief, of this unique work considered primarily as literature.

I have been interested in good books from childhood, and was brought up to appreciate fine English style. Thus it is by no means surprising that as I began to read *Science and Health* and have continued to study it daily over a period of many years, I should consider carefully not only its contents but also its standing as literature.

Its style is characterized by dignity, grace and clarity of expression. So far from being in any way limited or monotonous in her use of language, Mary Baker Eddy possessed an exceptionally wide vocabulary and used it to the full in her efforts to express, in the most vivid and accurate manner possible, the thoughts which thronged her ever-active consciousness. Rhythmic cadences reminiscent of the Psalms—whether in Hebrew or in English—are often to be found in her writings; but it is noteworthy that she was at pains never to subordinate depth of content to beauty of phrasing.

It is clear that she constantly bore in mind that she was writing a textbook, providing the explicit rules for practicing Christian Science, together with detailed descriptions and illustrations of its nature—but none of the many textbooks I have had occasion to study has ever equalled or even approached the effectiveness and impact of her strong, but beautifully turned sentences.

One of the most striking characteristics of Mary Baker Eddy's writing is her quiet but compelling sense of dominion and authority. It is almost as though she echoed unconsciously the oft-repeated *Koh amar Adonai*—"Thus saith the Lord!"—of the great Hebrew seers, who, like herself, were so assured that they had received a revelation from God Himself, that they had no hesitation in recording with force and dignity the thoughts which came to them.

The Discoverer of Christian Science possessed no false modesty with regard to the promises, warnings, statements and assurances which abound in *Science and Health*—feeling, as she did, that they were recorded through her rather than by her.

I suppose that not a few authors with a deep sense of mission and of inspiration have had the experience of feeling, on re-reading some of their most exalted statements, that they came from a power above and beyond themselves—so much so that they did not recall having penned them. With Mary Baker Eddy this was constantly the case, for she was assured that what she recorded had been revealed to her and that it was inspired by that divine Mind which she identified as God, Truth, and Love.

One interesting aspect of the growing recognition and widening acceptance of the Christian Science textbook is shown by the fact that several of our most widely known dictionaries, including Webster's New International, cite many of Mrs. Eddy's definitions for theological and religious terms.

William Dana Orcutt, himself an author of wide repute, and printer of *Science and Health* from 1897 to his passing in 1953, has set down for us his impression of Mary Baker Eddy's meeting in 1881 with John Wilson, his predecessor as head of the University Press in Cambridge, Massachusetts. After naming some of the illustrious New England writers whose books had been printed by this long established firm—including Oliver Wendell Holmes, Henry Wadsworth Longfellow, Nathaniel Hawthorne, John Greenleaf Whittier, Ralph Waldo Emerson, and James Russell Lowell, Mr. Orcutt writes (*Mary Baker Eddy and her Books:* p. 12):—"Little did John Wilson realize, that January afternoon, that the modest but confident little woman sitting at his desk was about to hand him the manuscript of a future classic which, in popularity, sales, and influence upon the world, would outrival the writings of any of the famous authors who had preceded her!"

FIFTEEN

THE MANUAL OF THE MOTHER CHURCH

THE BASIS of our church government is what is entitled
*Manual of The Mother Church, The First Church of Christ,
Scientist, in Boston, Massachusetts,* by Mary Baker Eddy.

In the early days of Christian Science it was Mrs. Eddy's
earnest hope and expectation that the system of healing and
salvation, of daily life and righteous action, which she had discovered and named, would be readily understood and accepted
and also that specific rules would be unnecessary. It soon became
apparent, however, that this was not the case. Even among her
own students, many of whom had but faintly grasped the meaning and obligations of the Science which she sought to unfold
to them, there arose misunderstandings and petty jealousies,
while in an excess of zeal, unwise steps were often taken. Thus
it became increasingly apparent that even those whose faithfulness and good intentions were beyond question, were in need
of rules to govern their conduct, as well as of statements to
clarify the *doctrine* of the faith she founded—using "doctrine"
in its original sense of "teaching." One might almost say that if
the Gospel (or "Good News") of Christian Science is supplied

by *Science and Health,* its Law is represented in that remarkable document known as the *Manual of The Mother Church.*

This *Manual* was further required as a result of the growth and wide spread of the Christian Science movement, in order that the church as a whole might have a uniform basis for its establishment, and at the same time, uniform rules for the satisfactory management of its affairs, together with wise guidance for the conduct of the individual members, especially, perhaps, in their dealings with others.

The *Manual of The Mother Church* holds its own unique place in the lives and affections of Christian Scientists. Like their Leader, Mary Baker Eddy, they turn reverently and constantly to the Bible, finding in it the basis and inspiration for the textbook of Christian Science, *Science and Health with Key to the Scriptures,* which she provided for them and which is their equally constant companion and guide. Never for a moment does it take the place of the Holy Scriptures, but it illumines and complements them, proving their practicality in everyday affairs, demonstrating the fact that the Master's promises of health, salvation and supply were intended to be taken literally, and showing how this could be accomplished.

The Bible and *Science and Health,* then, may be said to point the way to the growth, progress and regeneration of the individual, while to the *Manual of The Mother Church* falls the important task of co-ordinating the endeavors of each member of that church, and of stabilizing its world-wide organization. That, at least, is one aspect of the significance of the *Manual* although its contents cover a wide range of subjects, and are of value and aid to Christian Scientists in innumerable ways. Not only does it record By-Laws governing their personal conduct, but also it lays stress upon their responsibilities as good citizens of their respective countries and of the world.

In considering the work of any organization, it is natural that one should take into account not only its activities, but also the basic motives which lie behind them. This being the case, I believe the reader will find much that is thought-provoking in what Mary Baker Eddy terms "A Rule for Motives and Acts," which appears as Article viii, Section 1, of the *Manual of The Mother Church*. Because of its perennial significance, this rule is read aloud by the First Reader as a part of the Sunday service or services on the first Sunday of every month, both in The Mother Church in Boston, and in its branches around the world.

This compact instruction for disciplined thought reads as follows: "Neither animosity nor mere personal attachment should impel the motives or acts of the members of The Mother Church. In Science, divine Love alone governs man; and a Christian Scientist reflects the sweet amenities of Love, in rebuking sin, in true brotherliness, charitableness, and forgiveness. The members of this Church should daily watch and pray to be delivered from all evil, from prophesying, judging, condemning, counseling, influencing or being influenced erroneously."

If the implications of this rule were put into effect for the guidance and inspiration of individuals and nations alike, it could surely be of incalculable value in releasing world tensions and in preparing for the reign of "on earth peace, good will toward men."

The earnest desire to gain freedom from false judgment, unkind condemnation, ill-considered counsel, and the acceptance or exercise of wrongful influence, might well be the goal of any sincere religionist or humanitarian, whether or not he subscribes to the teachings of Christian Science, and accepts directly the wise rules laid down by Mary Baker Eddy for the guidance and protection of the members of her church.

The thought and practice of persistent prayer is brought out even more specifically in yet another of the By-Laws to be found in our *Church Manual* (Article viii; Section 4). Under the heading "Daily Prayer," Mrs. Eddy writes: "It shall be the duty of every member of this Church to pray each day: 'Thy kingdom come;' let the reign of divine Truth, Life, and Love be established in me, and rule out of me all sin; and may Thy Word enrich the affections of all mankind, and govern them!"

In applying this concept to the individual needs of the members of her Church, Mary Baker Eddy saw clearly the necessity of its acceptance by each one as a practical inner ruling of God, good, in his individual consciousness.

The thought of the value of permitting truly Godlike thinking and activity to have full play in the lives of men, has, of course, various parallels in the Bible, one of which is to be found in St. Paul's advice to the Colossians: "Let the peace of God rule in your hearts."

It is surely noteworthy that the final clause of this prayer reaches beyond the boundaries of the individual to consider the needs of humanity at large. True, the desire for the *enrichment* of the *affections* of mankind may seem to present an unusual approach to the coming of God's kingdom on earth, and yet, is it not the desires and affections of men which are apt to control their actions as well as their emotions?

Thus the prayer which Mary Baker Eddy established for daily use by all the members of the Church she founded, can be viewed not only as a contribution to the true progress of each individual accepting and practicing it, but also as yet another potent instrument for world peace.

Under the heading "Alertness to Duty" (*Manual:* Article viii; Section 6), Mrs. Eddy records a further important rule for the constant direction of Christian Scientists, which also contributes to their protection. "It shall be the duty of every member of this Church to defend himself daily against aggressive mental suggestion, and not be made to forget nor to neglect his duty to God, to his Leader, and to mankind. By his works he shall be judged,—and justified or condemned."

Although the vital implications of this By-Law are far too broad to be more than lightly touched upon here, perhaps, through it, those who are not familiar with this Science may be brought to glimpse one of the many aids provided for the student in his search for harmony and health.

The reader may naturally inquire as to the nature of these self-assertive mental arguments against which daily defense is requisite according to Christian Science. It may be replied that they come in many forms, some obvious, some insidious. A careful study of each word in the phrase *aggressive mental suggestion* may clarify its implications, but I know of nothing but Christian Science, understood and practiced, that is capable of nullifying its effects, and of offering the solution to the riddle of inharmony which it presents.

Only one very obvious example need be noted to illustrate the kind of bombardment which hourly attacks our thought.

At certain seasons of the year there may be a widespread prediction or suggestion that "colds" are to be expected. But just because some are troubled by this type of malady does not necessitate its spreading to others and reaching virtually epidemic proportions. Some, if they are sufficiently convinced that a cold is infectious, quite naturally feel the results of it; while others, equally convinced that they need not accept what they certainly do not want, repel the widely publicized suggestion regarding prevalent colds—and so remain free from them. This simple illustration could well be extended to refer to diseases and calamities commonly viewed as far more serious or dangerous than the so-called "common cold."

In their daily efforts to overcome such hypnotic suggestions in accord with the rule given them by the Founder of their denomination, Christian Scientists bear in mind certain basic facts laid down in the Bible and confirmed by the teachings and practice of Christian Science. Among these are the assurance that God is good, and that He loves His creation—both the universe and man—and governs it perpetually and harmoniously, and that it is the task and privilege of His children to recognize and claim this government in their individual experience. If God is indeed divine Mind, as the Scriptures imply, and as

Christian Science firmly maintains, erroneous and fear-promoting suggestions, no matter how aggressive they may appear to be, surely do not emanate from that Mind and consequently should not be accepted as real or effective, or even inevitable. A recognition of such facts as these helps to dispel harmful suggestions from any quarter, however innocent or well-intentioned they may appear.

The varied types of mesmeric suggestion, although unquestionably including those of physical disease or inharmony, are of course by no means limited to that field. Subtle arguments in the form of temptation, such as dishonesty, depravity or violence, must be and can be prevented from gaining a foothold in thought.

Suggestions of discouragement, depression, accident and limitation in countless forms, are all too familiar to the human race, and the value of regular self-defense against them, through prayer and spiritual perception, is surely beyond dispute. Here again innumerable antidotes against this species of mental poison can be found by deep study, in the light of Christian Science, of the triumphant experiences of patriarchs and prophets, and of Christ Jesus and his immediate followers.

On this firm Biblical basis, the Christian Science textbook, and the lives of individual Christian Scientists, present further illustrations showing how false suggestions can indeed be overcome in our own day.

Still other kinds of such erroneous suggestion are to be seen in malicious rumor, and in the general and often unconscious dissemination of fear—fear of disease, disaster, lack, unpopularity, etc.—through the press, radio, television and other means of communication.

More than half a century ago, Mrs. Eddy herself commented upon this tendency in the words: "Looking over the newspapers of the day, one naturally reflects that it is dangerous to live, so loaded with disease seems the very air. These descriptions carry fears to many minds, to be depicted in some future time upon the body." (*Miscellaneous Writings:* p. 7). Part of the task of *The Christian Science Journal* which she founded at that period, and of *The Christian Science Monitor,* which she established later, was to overcome such suggestions by the means of consistently constructive articles and news reports.

Realizing that the world, however reluctantly, is coming to accept the potentialities of Christian Science healing, we ourselves strive, ever more persistently, to prove in the midst of any situation, our awareness that the Christian Scientist has a duty to perform in overcoming through daily regeneration, all evidence of illness or accident. Moreover, in order to encourage others to trust God with their welfare, we accept the joyous privilege of dedicating ourselves to constant and unselfish vigilance.

Christ Jesus has commanded his followers to "be ... perfect" in order to reflect God, and has himself led the way. Mary Baker Eddy, at great cost, established the pattern of obedience in our modern world, realizing that all mankind is hungering for healing and for release from the innumerable woes resulting from its mortal fears.

In seeking conscientiously to heed the wise warning to protect their thoughts from insidious suggestions, together with the stipulation that they should pray daily for themselves and for the advancement of all mankind, and keep equally regular guard over their inmost motives and all the activities resulting therefrom, Christian Scientists set before them a high goal, but one which they feel to be not only desirable, but capable of attainment.

Apart from rules for the guidance of the individual members of The Mother Church, three of which I have quoted in the preceding pages, the *Manual* sets forth a remarkably detailed and comprehensive outline of the general government and procedure of our church organization, which contributes immeasurably to its success and to its cohesive force.

For example, it provides for the orderly and uniform conduct of all Christian Science services, stating the qualifications required of the Readers who conduct them and indicating the conditions under which membership in the organization is to be obtained and retained. The relationship between The Mother Church and its branches is also clearly defined. It is under the *Manual* that all the fundamental activities of our church are established and upheld on an orderly basis. Under the *Manual* the central administrative government of The Mother Church is vested in The Christian Science Board of Directors, while its vital publishing activities are entrusted to the care of a Board of Trustees. The work of our Committees on Publication finds its authorization in the Church Manual, which also provides expressly for the training of both children and adults in consonance with the teachings of Christian Science.

Many other aspects of the breadth and scope of this constitution of the Christian Science Church could be mentioned, but those which I have just briefly enumerated will perhaps serve to suggest to the reader its fundamental importance, not only as a digest of procedure but also of conduct, outlining rules and goals for the constant consideration of the alert student of this subject, with a view to assuring the firm and correct establishment of the Christian Science Church as a practical entity.

The By-Laws contained in the *Manual of The Mother Church* were gradually evolved by Mrs. Eddy as the movement she founded and established grew under her careful and prayerful guidance; thus they were wrought out on the anvil of practical experience. Each By-Law came in answer to a specific need, and her alert and ever receptive thought caught and held in precise phraseology the message required for the moment or that which she intuitively felt would be required to maintain the government of her church and the direction of its members in the future.

Just as Mary Baker Eddy could and did evaluate impersonally the deep significance and importance of the Christian Science textbook, so she recognized with equal clarity the value and the necessity of the *Manual of The Mother Church*. She was convinced that its provisions had come to her as the result of revelation, and that, as such, they possessed an innate authority which transcended her personal views or desires and which could not be overthrown. Hence, she had no hesitation in making this remarkable prophecy regarding this book: "Notwithstanding the sacrilegious moth of time, eternity awaits our Church Manual, which will maintain its rank as in the past, amid ministries aggressive and active, and will stand when those have passed to rest." (*Miscellany:* p. 230).

In view of Mrs. Eddy's forthright affirmation regarding the permanency of our Church Manual, it may interest the reader to know that in the year 1919, the authority of the Manual as a legal instrument governing the Christian Science Church was tested in the secular courts, and that its permanent validity was fully upheld and vindicated by the Supreme Judicial Court of the Commonwealth of Massachusetts. One of the bases of the plea of those who brought suit seems to have lain in their contention that because certain By-Laws in our Church Manual stated or implied that Mrs. Eddy's personal signature was required for their execution—therefore, with her passing, the whole instrument was invalidated.

After most thorough investigation of the whole matter, the Court ruled, in effect, that it was unquestionably Mrs. Eddy's intention, as shown by her published statements and under her will, that both The Mother Church and the *Manual* should remain in effect in perpetuity. Moreover it was made clear that when, as the result of her passing, she could no longer provide the personal signature mentioned in certain passages, the next in authority under the By-Laws—The Christian Science Board of Directors—could legally function on her behalf.

While the alleged reason for the suit had been to dispute and lessen the authority of The Christian Science Board of Directors and increase that of the Board of Trustees of The Christian Science Publishing Society, its effects—if it had been allowed by the Court—would have been to impair seriously the authority of the Church Manual, together with the structure of the whole organization of the Christian Science Church.

Actually, the unequivocal decision of the Court upholding Mrs. Eddy's original plan had the effect of fully supporting both the authority of the *Manual* and the permanence of The Mother Church itself, confirming on the basis of secular law the spiritual foundation of which she had always been convinced.

SIXTEEN

THE "NEW TONGUE" OF
CHRISTIAN SCIENCE

IN THE sixteenth chapter of Mark's Gospel, Christ Jesus
designates speaking "with new tongues" as one of the "signs"
which would follow "them that believe"—not only in his own
day, but in all time to come.

One implication of the Master's words may well be that the
progressive development of spiritual thinking which he clearly
anticipated would of necessity require new modes of expression,
even as his own teaching and interpretation of the Ten Commandments reached far above and beyond the specific phrases
traditionally recorded by Moses. Moreover, Jesus' familiar parable
concerning the unwisdom of attempting to contain new wine in
old wineskins, would seem to point in the same direction. Both
his words and his works brought out the inner significance of
the only *Bible* available to him—the Old Testament—giving
new and vital meanings to its often somewhat obscure statements.

In our own day, Mary Baker Eddy has endeavored with marked
success to clarify and explain the Bible passages still further, for
modern ears, and in application to problems of today. Thus we
find her stating that "The spiritual sense of the Scriptures brings

out the scientific sense, and is the new tongue referred to in the last chapter of Mark's Gospel." (*Science and Health:* p. 272). Wrestling with deeply spiritual ideas, which to many seemed new and strange, she searched for words with which to explain her meaning. She had, of necessity, to develop new terms, or, more generally, to clothe old terms with new implications, in an effort to interpret the language of Spirit. Well might she have echoed the words of Christ Jesus himself, when he cried "Why do ye not understand my speech? even because ye cannot hear my word." (John 8:43)

It is obvious that certain words or phrases used with special meanings must be grasped if one is to obtain a workable understanding of any given subject. Christian Science is no exception to this rule, and while it would be manifestly impractical to provide any complete list or detailed description of words and phrases used in a special sense by Mrs. Eddy and by Christian Scientists in general, it may be of interest to the reader if I mention a few at this point, which were unfamiliar to me when I first took up the study of Christian Science, and which have not been discussed to any extent in earlier chapters.

One such phrase, for example, is *animal magnetism*. While relatively unfamiliar today, it appears to have been widely used at the time when *Science and Health* first appeared, in 1875, and is virtually synonymous with mesmerism or hypnotism, as Mrs. Eddy herself points out. Realizing the importance of being alert to the nature and alleged effects of this so-called force or influence, she devoted the fifth chapter of her textbook to a discussion of the subject, as already noted, exposing its inherent fallacies under the title "Animal Magnetism Unmasked."

Christian Scientists often use the phrase animal magnetism as providing an effective summation of false or wrongful influence in all its forms—as describing an alleged force drawing or driving the individual *downward*, or *backward*, away from right thinking or action. The word *animal* is construed as indicating that such attraction is neither constructive nor spiritual, but simply animal or carnal in character and effect.

There are conceded to be two main types of animal magnetism. *Malicious* animal magnetism implies any direct or conscious effort to mislead, deceive or subvert the individual. *Ignorant* animal magnetism, perhaps less obvious and for that reason sometimes ignored, indicates the unconscious deception of incorrect or negative thinking in general, resulting in inharmony and confusion.

Can there be any defense against animal magnetism, mesmerism, or hypnotism in all their menacing forms and subtle disguises, excepting in the firm and persistent assurance that the only true attraction is that which draws *upward* or *forward* towards God, complete good; spirituality, health and progress, counteracting by its very nature, evil, materiality, disease and retrogression; and, above all, that the only real control is that exercised by the divine Mind, God, good, and forever applicable to His spiritual creation, man?

One of the advantages of using the term *error* to describe whatever is opposed to the nature of God and to the true nature of man as His reflection, is that error implies, first, the need for, and, second, the possibility of correction. The very existence of the term error implies a standard of truth to which the thought or situation can be made to conform.

The young student of arithmetic may put down 2 plus 2 equals 5, but his error can be readily corrected by erasing the 5 and replacing it with a 4, in accordance with the fundamental laws of mathematics. When he has thus returned to the correct and universally accepted standard in that field of study, the error vanishes, no matter how many people may have been persuaded to believe the error to be true, for no amount of abuse or misuse of a mathematical rule can possibly disprove it.

Christian Science maintains that anything opposed to the divine standard or Principle of perfect Mind is justly classified as *error*, whether it appears as disease, lack, stagnation, sin, or any other form of inharmony, and that when the required correction is made on the basis of God's standard of perfection, the error or misconception disappears.

God's law of health, perfection, abundance, has never changed in any least degree. His Truth is established and invariable. Thus Christian Science demonstrates that when the error in our thinking is corrected by a joyous acceptance of the truth of being, the results are manifested in terms of our human experience in health, harmony, abundance and progress.

In short, when Christian Scientists use the term "error" this constitutes a tacit affirmation of the existence and permanent validity of Truth, an acknowledgment of the fact that whatever the error seems to be, it is not real and that it can be corrected.

In view of the stress which we lay upon the concept of God not only as Truth, but as Mind, forever perfect, immortal, un-limited—Mind the supreme universal intelligence, which governs and directs man and confers the understanding which is his birthright as the child of God—it is natural that we should also refer by way of contrast to *mortal mind*. This does not, of course, mean that we consider "mortal mind" as real, in spite of all its pretensions to reality and power. Rather it is viewed as the alleged antithesis of God, good, health and harmony. Its claims are as false as they are manifold.

Christian Science argues that since Mind, God, is immortal, all-inclusive, the term *mortal mind* epitomizes the various false theories and beliefs about God and man which seek to obtrude upon the consciousness of mankind. In fact, every erroneous thought or argument which appears in the form of sickness or sin, dissension or inharmony, dishonesty or discord of any kind, is viewed as a manifestation of this self-contradictory concept *mortal mind*—a false theory which can be ruled out by a steadfast recognition of the deathless reality and omnipotent power of Mind—the ever-living God.

What the Christian Scientist terms *mortal mind* often comes remarkably close to that personified representation of all evil influences, commonly known as the devil.

The basic fallacy of mortal mind lies in its mortality, since by its derivation the term *mortal* indicates that which is subject to death. Hence it is devoid of stability and permanence. Its very name implies its destruction. While the specific phrase does not occur in the Bible records, the apostle Paul appears to have prepared directly for Mrs. Eddy's thought on this subject by his reference to the unreasoning vanity of the "fleshly mind," and particularly by his statement to the effect that "the carnal mind is enmity against God." (Rom. 8:7). Whatever constitutes active opposition to God, good, is obviously to be avoided and resisted, thus it will be readily understood why it is that Christian Scientists do all in their power to overcome that compendium of false thinking and acting which they describe as *mortal mind*.

Sometimes reference may be made to any kind of sickness or disease as a *claim*, thus reflecting the assurance that such inharmonies are neither real nor God-sanctioned, and still less God-bestowed, but simply assume or *claim* a reality and importance which in no way belongs to them. The recipe for overcoming false claims is set forth by Mrs. Eddy in *Science and Health* (p. 390), where she urges her readers to see to it that any such claim does not become established or strengthened in their thinking, and to do away with it promptly and effectively. "Suffer no claim of sin or of sickness to grow upon the thought. Dismiss it with an abiding conviction that it is illegitimate, because you know that God is no more the author of sickness than He is of sin."

In business and other fields it is not unusual for a firm or individual to be faced with claims of various types and often of large proportions. It is, of course, standard practice for the fairness, justice and legality of such claims to be carefully weighed before their validity is admitted. Now, in the field of health, is there anything either fair or just about the claim of sickness, which automatically implies the exercise of a power and authority greater than that of God, the source of all good, the creator of all harmony? Christian Science maintains that the claims of sin and sickness are fundamentally false, and therefore are to be vigorously challenged. They are claims, yes—but that is all they are, claims and not realities, for they have no authority under God's law.

Closely connected with this special usage of the term *claim* is our description of sickness or disease as a *belief,* but this does not mean that Christian Scientists blandly or scornfully ignore such problems. Still less do they adopt a supercilious or "holier-than-thou" attitude towards those who, to their own discomfort, firmly hold and sometimes even cherish, such beliefs. Mrs. Eddy makes this clear in many passages, emphasizing the ever-present need for true compassion combined with Christian healing.

We realize that many do accept such conditions as inevitable, as sincerely as they do tenaciously, but we are concerned to maintain that, scientifically considered, apart from the personal problem involved, sickness is simply a *belief,* however firmly held, a phase or phenomenon of deterioration, which may be expected to develop as long as man accepts the premise that he is material or proceeds from matter, with its indigenous process of decay or corruption. To the extent that we accept it as having power, necessity and justification, such a belief affects us physically or mentally, as the case may be.

Healing results when our belief in inharmony is replaced by the understanding that it has neither source nor power, because God, Spirit, the source of all harmony, governs every aspect of His spiritual creation at all times and under all conditions, maintaining the universe, including man, at the standpoint of perfection. Healing, after all, is surely the acceptance of the unescapable harmony of man as the beloved child of God. Healing of thought precedes and assures healing of the physical body and its inharmonies, for, as the Bible says regarding man, "as he thinketh in his heart, so is he."

Among students of Christian Science one constantly hears

references to *demonstration,* a word which we use to describe a practical proof of our recognition of the power of God in human experience. Spiritual understanding and purity of thought further and contribute to the working out of such proofs, which indicate that there is no more uncertainty in our seeing and accepting these *demonstrations* than in the source from which they come—God's perpetual goodness and grace.

Every salesman is familiar with the value of giving a demonstration of his product, showing its good points and how it works, thereby establishing a demand for it, first in the thoughts of individual prospects, and gradually in the community.

A Christian Science demonstration exemplifies the practical effectiveness of this system of divine healing in contributing to progress and unfoldment as well as in overcoming some one or more of the numerous types of inharmony—mental, physical, moral, financial, etc.—which present themselves in the course of human existence.

Such a *demonstration,* then, is a proof, which may be large or small, spectacular or simple, of the efficacy of Christian Science, *first,* because it is Christian, and *second,* because it is both practical and scientific, and therefore demonstrable.

CONCLUSION

MARY BAKER EDDY, in spite of her monumental task of founding, leading, establishing and promoting the spread of a world-wide religious movement, was remarkably successful in keeping alert to the events and problems of our nation and of the world. Following her example, members of her church do not limit their interests and experience to the strictly religious field, but are to be found taking active part in all fields of constructive endeavor.

One reason for this is the fact that, as I have already mentioned, Christian Science is not exclusively a religion, nor even primarily a method of healing disease. It does fulfill these requirements of the individual, but it goes farther in that it is inherently a way of living and, as such, is applicable to and helpful in all walks of life, from the humblest to the most responsible. Dealing essentially with God's law and His government, and interpreting Him as Principle, it provides a firm and logical basis for legal and governmental activities of high caliber.

As Mrs. Eddy has written (*Science and Health:* p. 128), "The term Science, properly understood, refers only to the laws of God and to His government of the universe, inclusive of man.

From this it follows that business men and cultured scholars have found that Christian Science enhances their endurance and mental powers, enlarges their perception of character, gives them acuteness and comprehensiveness and an ability to exceed their ordinary capacity." This has certainly been my observation and experience in both business and professional life.

Christian Scientists have the interests of humanity at heart, and are eager to contribute of their best to the good of society and of their fellow men, while they are meticulous in their obedience to and respect for the law of the land.

It may be recorded here that Mrs. Eddy's attitude towards war was a realistic one. Although deeply interested in peace, and active in at least one peace organization, she was not a pacifist. While advocating peaceful means for solving conflict whether between individuals or nations, her strong position concerning the active participation which would be expected of her followers in times of national emergency of any kind is very clear in her writings.

Thus in time of war Christian Scientists throughout the world have been in no way behind other good citizens in performing an active role in the armed services of their country, while Wartime Ministers and other workers, together with Commissioned Chaplains of our denomination, have done much not only for members of their own faith, but also to aid and comfort many others in need of support and encouragement in such circumstances. The breadth and results of such work and of the war relief associated with it, have been recorded in *The Story of Christian Science Wartime Activities 1939-1946*—a book of over 400 pages. Then, too, the record of our church in promptly establishing and loyally maintaining funds to provide supplies and financial aid for those in need in time of flood, hurricane or other disasters at home or abroad, is well known. Our attitude in any emergency is to cling steadfastly to the truth of God's eternal and unceasing government regardless of the evidence before the physical senses.

While maintaining the fundamental unreality of disease, sin, death, disaster and matter itself, we are fully aware of the fact that countless thousands of our fellow men remain in bondage to their own fears, either because they are unaware of the freedom which Christian Science offers, or are as yet unready or unwilling to accept it. We do not ignore, and still less despise, their difficulties, but do all in our power to alleviate them, meeting our neighbors on the level of their understanding and acceptance. We have a great gift to share—the ever-practical gift of Christian Science—but are at pains not in any way to enforce it upon others. Our honest and sincere efforts to practice it daily provide its most effective introduction.

The Bible assures us that "There is no respect of persons with God." Indeed how could God, as divine Principle, Life, Truth, Love, in any way exercise favoritism or partiality? His loving care extends to man as man. Our task, then, surely lies in the realization and acceptance of His infinite bounty, offered freely to all. Naturally the rate of progress varies with different individuals. Equally naturally, in the consideration of Christian Science, some may be delayed by environment, background, or early training, but its logical approach, based on the Scriptures and on a practical acceptance of their teachings concerning God, and of the duties, privileges and responsibilities devolving on man as His reflection, cannot fail to impress the honest inquirer.

I well remember an incident which occurred many years ago, when I, as a salesman in a mid-western state, called upon a clergyman in my territory. Somehow the subject of Christian Science arose, and we stood in the middle of his study floor for an hour, while he asked questions and I answered them to the best of my ability. Doubtless still bound by his ordination vows, he was not prepared at that time to accept the conclusions I had already reached, but he was impressed by the logic of the points I made. His parting words, as I recall them, were: "Young man, I cannot agree with what you say, but I must admit that your arguments are logical!"

In that instance logic provided the point of interest or of contact. Another may be first impressed by the healing of a friend; still another by some specific aspect of Christian Science teaching of which he has been informed. No matter what the avenue of approach may be, it leads to a study which I, for one, have found to be infinitely inspiring and rewarding, as well as intensely practical. While such a study is endless and in my own case has already continued for a considerable number of years, resulting in increased understanding and ever renewed interest, even my earliest studies brought progress and enlightenment.

Let me repeat that the innumerable physical healings wrought on the basis of a Christianly scientific approach to the wonderful works of the prophets, of Christ Jesus and of his immediate followers, represent but one aspect—however important—of the benefits accruing from the study and practice of Christian Science. When physical cure is brought about and even before that occurs in our experience, how vital and encouraging is the continual increase in our capacity to understand the power of God and to see the enriching results of this understanding in our experience!

One cannot read any of the many articles and books in current circulation relating to the mental nature of disease and the need of treatment from this point of view, without being aware in some degree of the penetrating and undeniable impact upon world thought of the discovery of Christian Science. The sturdy adherence to its teachings by multitudes who have proved its effects in their own experience, has fostered a wholesome spirit of rebellion against the acceptance by mankind of the inevitability of any kind of doom. Although this contribution may never be fully evaluated, its leavening and vitalizing influence has been felt and will continue to express itself in the evolution of human thinking.

Mary Baker Eddy's original hope and plan was to introduce her concept of Christianity to the orthodox churches, with the confident expectation that they would readily accept and incorporate it. It was not long, however, before she discovered that the various denominations with which she was in contact were inclined to reject this apparently new idea, turning a deaf ear to the clear promise of freedom ringing through the teachings and practice of the Science of Christianity.

Eager though she was to have Christian Science and its blessings speedily accepted by all Christendom, she was not unaware of the phases through which it must pass, for on page 104 of *Science and Health,* she quotes Agassiz, the naturalist, as follows: " 'Every great scientific truth goes through three stages. First, people say it conflicts with the Bible. Next, they say it has been discovered before. Lastly, they say they have always believed it.' "

Mary Baker Eddy was impelled, therefore, as we have seen, to establish her own church, *The First Church of Christ, Scientist.* With its original members and indeed with all mankind, she was prepared at all costs to share the ever widening horizons of spiritual unfoldment which she envisioned. This great spiritual Leader's expectation of good reached beyond national and international frontiers. In her textbook she offers an inspired challenge to every citizen to accept as his own "the glorious liberty of the children of God" of which Paul the apostle speaks. The breadth of her kindly interest in the welfare of all humanity shines forth again and again in her writings, and she recognized no inequality of opportunity in the reception of the blessings resulting from her contribution to the world.

It is evident, then, that Mary Baker Eddy's interests were broad, wide and compassionate. Her thoughts and prayers reached far beyond the borders of her own followers, her own church, to envision the steady progress and eventual regeneration and redemption of all mankind. Love was her central motive. Love, as God, was the source of the mission of healing and enlightenment which she performed on the basis of revelation and of the Master's words and works. The Discoverer of Christian Science concludes a chapter in *Science and Health with Key to the Scriptures* (p. 55), with the following remarkable passage, which helps to re-emphasize *"Why I am a Christian Scientist"*:

> "Truth's immortal idea is sweeping down the centuries, gathering beneath its wings the sick and sinning. My weary hope tries to realize that happy day, when man shall recognize the Science of Christ and love his neighbor as himself,—when he shall realize God's omnipotence and the healing power of the divine Love in what it has done and is doing for mankind. The promises will be fulfilled. The time for the reappearing of the divine healing is throughout all time; and whosoever layeth his earthly all on the altar of divine Science, drinketh of Christ's cup now, and is endued with the spirit and power of Christian healing.
>
> "In the words of St. John: 'He shall give you another Comforter, that he may abide with you *forever.*' This Comforter I understand to be Divine Science."

BIBLIOGRAPHY

(1) Works of Mary Baker Eddy

(Published by the Trustees under the Will of Mary Baker Eddy)

Science and Health with Key to the Scriptures
Manual of The Mother Church
Miscellaneous Writings
Retrospection and Introspection
Unity of Good
Pulpit and Press
Rudimental Divine Science
No and Yes
Christian Science versus Pantheism
Messages to The Mother Church: June 1900, 1901 and 1902
Christian Healing
The People's Idea of God
The First Church of Christ, Scientist, and Miscellany
Poems, including "Christ and Christmas"

Concordance to Science and Health and Other Writings

239

(2) THE CHRISTIAN SCIENCE PERIODICALS

(Founded by Mary Baker Eddy and published by
The Christian Science Publishing Society)

The Christian Science Journal: Monthly in English

Christian Science Sentinel: Weekly in English

The Herald of Christian Science: Monthly in French, German,
and English-Braille. Quarterly in Dutch, Danish, Norwegian,
Swedish, Italian, Portuguese and Spanish.

Christian Science Quarterly: Quarterly in English, Danish,
Dutch, French, German, Norwegian, Spanish, Swedish and
English-Braille.

The Christian Science Monitor: Daily, except Sundays and
holidays, in English.

(3) BIOGRAPHIES OF MARY BAKER EDDY
AND OTHER BOOKS RELATING TO CHRISTIAN SCIENCE

(Published by The Christian Science Publishing Society)

Armstrong, Joseph: *The Mother Church*

Christian Science Hymnal

Hay, Ella H.: *A Child's Life of Mary Baker Eddy*

Johnston, Julia Michael: *Mary Baker Eddy: Her Mission and
Triumph*

Orcutt, William Dana: *Mary Baker Eddy and Her Books*

Powell, Lyman P.: *Mary Baker Eddy: A Life Size Portrait*

Ramsay, E. Mary: *Christian Science and Its Discoverer*

Smith, Clifford P.: *Historical Sketches*

The Story of Christian Science Wartime Activities: 1939-1946

Tomlinson, Irving C.: *Twelve Years with Mary Baker Eddy*

We Knew Mary Baker Eddy

We Knew Mary Baker Eddy (Second and Third Series)

Wilbur, Sibyl: *The Life of Mary Baker Eddy*

Williamson, Margaret: *The Mother Church Extension*

(Published by Houghton Mifflin Company)

Canham, Erwin D.: *Commitment to Freedom: The Story of
"The Christian Science Monitor"*

INDEX

A

absent treatment, 125-133
accidents overcome, 63, 80, 127-133, 171, 188, 190f., 221f.
advertising, 137, 143f.
Agassiz, Louis, 237
aggressive mental suggestion, 132, 219-222
Alertness to Duty, 219-222
allness of God, 69, 75, 104, 108, 110f., 212
American Standard Version, 176f.
animal magnetism, 211, 227f.
antidote, 43, 125, 221
ascension, 92, 102f.
associations, students', 162f.
atomic energy, etc., 106f.
atonement, 100-104, 211
at-one-ment, 63, 102
Authorized Version, 34, 36, 46, 56, 67, 173-177 etc., *passim; see also* King James Version

B

Baker, Abigail Ambrose, 179
Baker, Albert, 179-181
Baker, Mark, 178f., 181
Baker, Mary Morse, 178, 182, 184f., 189
Bancroft, Samuel P., 154
baptism, 15, 84-87, 91

Beatitudes, 86, 164
belief, 231
Bergson, Henri, 105
Bible, The, *see* Chap. XI, 170-177; also 14, 16f., 59f., 94, 104, 112, 181, 205, 207, 217 etc., *passim*
Bible courses, author's, 38, 49, 174
Bible Lesson Committee, 70, 77, 82
Bow, N. H., 178f.
Braille, 136, 138
branch churches, 91, 163, 166, 223; democratic, 66, 170, 196f.
building of Original Mother Church, 194f., 198; Extension, 198

C

Canada, 18, 149, 199
capitalization, 33f., 40, 48, 54
Catechism, Westminster; Shorter, 31, 118, 181; Larger, 84
Charitable Institutions, 201
charter, 157, 166, 192-196
Christ Jesus, Son of God, 22, 96f.; Master-Christian, 67, 87, 132, 172, 190; Messiah, 86, 97, 113f.; Physician, 63f., 92, 99, 113-116, 126, 188, 204; Saviour, 96, 102-104; Teacher, 35f., 41, 51, 64, 96, 98, 121; Wayshower, 44, 104, 116, 118, 156
Christian Science Board of Directors, The, 66, 139, 145f., 158f., 195, 199, 223f.

241